Teaching Problem Solving
in Vocational Education

An important aim for vocational education and training in both the school and post-school sector is the development of thinking skills, which are necessary for the flexible and adaptable performance of work tasks. Problem-solving skills are among the key competences which make up the new vocational qualifications, and this book is designed to offer guidelines to teachers and lecturers involved in teaching those skills.

Drawing on cognitive theories about learning and problem solving, Rebecca Soden argues that thinking processes cannot be detached from the context in which they are being applied. Thinking skills, therefore, are most effectively developed along with vocational competences and not as separate add-on courses. The book offers suggestions on how students develop thinking processes which will enhance their learning of information and their skill in applying it in subsequent problem solving, and looks at the problems many encounter in the transfer of learning. Sections of instructional plans show how the techniques work in practice, and there is also advice on how to assess problem solving.

Dr Rebecca Soden, a chartered psychologist, is Senior Lecturer at the Scottish School of Further Education, Strathclyde University.

Teaching Problem Solving in Vocational Education

Rebecca Soden

London and New York

First published 1994
by Routledge
11 New Fetter Lane, London EC4P 4EE

Simultaneously published in the USA and Canada
by Routledge
29 West 35th Street, New York, NY 10001

Typeset in Palatino by
Ponting–Green Publishing Services, Chesham, Bucks
Printed and bound in Great Britain by
TJ Press (Padstow) Ltd, Padstow, Cornwall

British Library Cataloguing in Publication Data
A catalogue record for this book is available from the
British Library.

Library of Congress Cataloging-in-Publication Data.
Soden, Rebecca
  Teaching problem solving in vocational
  education/Rebecca Soden.
      p.   cm.
  Includes bibliographical references and index.
  1. Thought and thinking–Study and teaching.
  2. Problem solving–Study and teaching.
  3. Vocational education.   I. Title.
  LB1590.3.S56   1994
  370.15'24–dc20   93–39846

  ISBN 0–415–09245–0 (hbk)
  ISBN 0–415–09246–9 (pbk)

For Joe

Contents

Activities

Figures

Preface

There is widespread agreement that the development of thinking skills which will improve learning and problem-solving performance at work is an important aim for vocational education and training. Books based on cognitive research on learning and problem solving often disappoint vocational education and training practitioners, who rightly want to know how cognitive insights fit with those derived from their own experience. They particularly want to see ideas illustrated in examples from their own vocational specialism.

The book was strongly influenced by psychology seminars with lecturers in Scottish further education colleges, many of whom found that psychological ideas, when synthesised with their own insights about learning, significantly illuminated their instructional practices. It became clear that there was a dearth of books which focused on psychological ideas which had substantial mileage for vocational education and training practitioners; provided brief explanations which can be quickly assimilated; and demonstrated how the ideas could enhance both problem-solving performance and learning strategies in vocational education.

I am grateful to all the lecturers in post-school education who made direct and indirect contributions to the book. Some of the more direct contributors were:

Caroline McCallum at Ayr College (Chapter 8)
Mairearad Kirkland at Bell College (Chapter 10)
Barbara Nelson at Dundee College (Chapter 5)
Russell McAllister at Motherwell College (Chapter 9)
Martin Macdonald at Glasgow Caledonian University (Chapter 9)
Jemima Magna at Fife College (Chapter 9)

Lynn Wallace at Queen Margaret College, Edinburgh (Chapters 5 and 9), and
Fiona Birse at Banff and Buchan College (Chapter 6).

I am grateful also to Stuart Niven, Director of the Scottish School of Further Education, who has supported me in so many ways. My colleague Sandra Little spent many weekends keying in the text and sustaining me with her wit. Helen Fairlie, my commissioning editor, provided invaluable guidance and support. Lively debate with HMCI Ron Tuck at the Scottish Office Education Department was useful in clarifying ideas. In 1986 John Nisbett and Janet Shucksmith let me see a draft of their 'Learning Strategies' which was to become highly acclaimed, and convinced me that vocational education also would benefit from a psychologically based approach to developing learning and problem-solving skills.

I would like to express my thanks to Nigel Blagg Associates for pre-publication access to their 'Thinking Skills at Work' (TSAW) Modules. I am indebted to the Employment Department, Sheffield, for allowing me to incorporate pages 69–71 from *Learning in Context*, by A. Wolf, J. Fotheringham and A. Grey (1990), *Research and Development*, 58, The Training Agency, Moorfoot, Sheffield, and excerpts from *Thinking and Learning at Work* (autumn 1993), produced by Nigel Blagg and Rachel Lewis.

I am also indebted to MENSA for permission to reproduce two problems they used in advertisements in the *Guardian*; to the *Herald* whose Mind Game appears in Chapter 5; and to Cambridge University Press, who allowed me to reproduce the selection task (Psychology Exhibition, Science Museum, 1977) which appears in Figure 1, page 120 of their publication entitled *Readings in Cognitive Science*, P.N. Johnson-Laird, and P.C. Wason (eds) (1977).

Chapter 1

Thinking matters at work

There was a time when the dividing lines were clear between jobs which needed thinking workers and ones which were so routinised that thinking was an unnecessary and even unhelpful skill. All of you who are involved in planning and delivering vocational education and training programmes know that more people than ever before are expected to be able to adjust their performance to accommodate everyday variations in task demands. Faced with a non-standard task or situation, they should be able to respond effectively. This helps define an important aim for vocational education and training in both the school and post-school sector. This aim is the development of thinking skills which are necessary and sufficient for flexible and adaptable performance of work tasks. Such skills also enhance learning, thereby offering the potential to improve levels of achievement. The notion of 'vocational A levels' implies a vocational curriculum which develops complex thinking skills.

This book will focus on those thinking operations which are most useful in skilled jobs in areas as diverse as catering, caring, engineering and business studies. These jobs and many others mentioned in the following chapters employ many thousands of people. To get their work done all of these people must work to agreed national standards and develop vocational competences. The best of workers, whether they be manual, technical, administrative, professional, scientific or managerial people, have gained skills in problem solving. This book provides guidelines for teaching those problem-solving skills.

Derived from cognitive theories about learning and problem solving, and from five research projects recently funded by the Employment Department, these guidelines will assist further education lecturers, teachers caught up in the increasing trend to vocationalise secondary education, and managers who have some role in facilitating the development of people.

In every occupational area thousands of people, of all ages and various experiences, are now seeking National Vocational Qualifications (NVQs). Increasingly, thinking skills are being emphasised. A traditional view of reasoning is of mental processes that can be tapped independently of the situation which is being reasoned about. An alternative recent view is that there are no such things as thinking processes detached from the context in which they are being applied. Rather, the information which people use in reasoning about situations and the form of the reasoning are inseparable. The practical significance of this alternative view (on which this book is based) is that thinking skills are most effectively developed along with vocational competences and not as the separate 'add-on' courses which have been popular in schools and colleges. The problems in Figure 1.1 from different occupational areas illustrate the diversity of contexts in which thinking skills are applied.

The last problem was drawn from an experiment carried out during 1992 when staff in a number of Laura Ashley stores were

---

Figure 1.1 Problems in different areas

1 The lunches in a factory canteen are due to be served at 12 noon and are nearly ready at 11.00 a.m. when there is a power cut. How is this situation to be managed?
2 A fourteen-month-old child on a social worker's care load has over the last three months sustained several injuries which may be non-accidental. The members present at a case conference must decide what action is to be taken.
3 A hollow shaft of 200 mm outside diameter and 100 mm inside diameter is used to transmit power with a torque rating of 73.63 kNm. You have to determine the angle of twist in radians for a length of shaft. Take the modules of rigidity to be 80 GN/m^2.
4 A financial services consultant has to advise a client on whether to sell £20,000 of units in a UK growth trust and use the proceeds to buy Scottish Power shares.
5 You have to decide whether to accept the endowment policy savings plan recommended by a salesman.
6 Ways of improving profits in a number of Laura Ashley stores have to be found.

given a free hand in solving the problem, with cash incentives linked to profits. Results were so much better than anticipated that the scheme is being developed. Reasoning by branch staff about increasing their own branch profits may be particularly effective because no one has had more practice than these employees in reasoning with the strands of information peculiar to that branch.

Effective financial consultants dealing with problem (4) above would reason with the technical information which is accumulated by competent practitioners. Out of this information would arise questions which are particularly effective for solving problems in this domain. They might, for example, ask about social, political and economic factors which currently, or in the near future, will influence both the costs of producing electricity and the price which can be obtained for the electricity. They would also ask questions about price/earnings ratios and dividend cover for the investments being considered. In tackling problem (5), questions need to be asked such as:

'What charges will be made for managing my money?'
'How much commission will you earn by selling me a policy?'
'Can I lose money under *any* circumstances?'
'Why should I give you my money rather than the building society?'

The canteen power cut described in problem (1) is discussed in Chapter 8, pages 142–3 and you will find a solution to problem (3) in Chapter 9.

These problems illustrate that thinking is closely bound up with what is being thought about. Central to thinking is interrogation of our own knowledge (in memory), a process which can both release information needed to solve problems and enable missing knowledge to be created. This relationship between thinking and information on which the thinking is based helps to explain the finding that people who are avid race-goers can solve complex problems when they are reasoning with race-track information but often cannot apply similar reasoning operations to problems outside the context of the race-track. This is not to say that people cannot learn to apply reasoning operations which they have learned in one situation to another, but that transfer is more problematic than is often implied in popular accounts of problem solving.

The distinctiveness of the approach lies in its synthesis of various findings in cognitive psychology to produce guidelines on teaching occupational problem-solving skills. These skills are gained in the course of imparting vocational knowledge rather than being taught in a separate, generic problem-solving course. What distinguishes this approach is its central idea (derived from Vygotsky's work) that any instructional activity can, and should, have a dual focus. First, it must of course contribute to achievement of the targeted competence. It is the second focus which is mostly neglected. This is the teaching of thinking skills which are inextricably linked with competences.

This book describes how you can adapt your existing strategies to achieve this extra yield. In this approach you analyse the mental processes which underlie learning and problem solving in your own occupational area. Drawing on the principles and illustrations in this book you can introduce these processes with the vocational content at each training session, and ensure that all practice includes practice in using these thinking skills. Integrated into the book are the well-researched messages which emerged from five recent Employment Department funded projects, one of which was carried out by the book's author. The approach is sufficiently student-centred to satisfy the most progressive educator, systematic enough to win the enthusiasm of the most traditional, while its potential for reducing training costs attracts the support of employers.

Crucial to your success is understanding that the central feature of the approach is development of the learners' insight into the nature of thinking and not merely formation of efficient thinking procedures for particular types of problems. If the approach seems 'teacher-centred' in places, this is because the mental processes required for learning and problem solving have to be taught systematically and not left to chance. A moment's thought will convince you that being able to ask appropriate questions is an important element in professional competency and that this aspect of competency has to be practised. For example, unless you have been exposed to systematic instruction in chemistry it is unlikely that you can ask questions which will lead to the solution of problems. Yet learning to learn and think is left to chance.

Post-school vocational education and training are vocational in the sense that they are specifically concerned with preparation for or improving performance in particular occupational areas. Vocational competences are accredited by the award of National Vocational Qualifications (NVQs) and their Scottish equivalents

(SVQs) at different levels. Traditionally, vocational education and training programmes leading to lower-level qualifications, the precursors of the present NVQ levels 1 and 2, were intended to equip people to carry out routine occupational tasks quickly and accurately, whereas higher-level programmes (degrees, HNCs) were intended to equip people to deal with tasks of a more complex and varied nature which would require good thinking skills. Changes in the nature of work have led to increasing recognition that most workers need to be thinking workers. 'All education and training provision should be structured and designed to develop self-reliance, flexibility and broad competence as well as specific skills' (CBI 1990). Wolf and Silver (1993) state that 'broad skills . . . . are the thinking and problem solving skills underlying competences . . . together with critical job specific knowledge'.

The introduction of General NVQs reflects a significant move towards more broad-based training and the promotion of transferable skills. As noted on page 6 problem solving, which is a behavioural manifestation of efficient thinking, is one of the 'core skills' in the NVQ Framework for Core Skills. The approach in this book is relevant also to the development of the other core skills – communication, numeracy, information technology and interpersonal effectiveness – which are also manifestations of thinking. Despite the obvious point that thinking processes underlie these competences, much instructional effort focuses on performance of tasks with little regard for developing the intellectual processes underlying performance. Blagg *et al.* (1993) comment, 'In spite of good intentions even more able trainees with NVQs at levels 1 and 2 remain inflexible and unresourceful when faced with the unfamiliar.'

Given this neglect of thinking skills, it is perhaps not surprising that there is good evidence from various sources that people are not very good problem solvers in practical situations. Edward de Bono reports: 'the many hours of tape recording that we have listened to at the Cognitive Research Trust suggest that the standard of thinking of many pupils is appallingly low. In the more able pupils this is obscured by an articulate style.' He concludes that 'most schools do not teach thinking at all'. Similar evidence comes from research in the post-school setting. In 'Six years on', the Scottish Office Education Department report on National Certificate programmes, it is noted that 'while examples were found of programmes with a strong emphasis on problem solving', this was not characteristic of the system.

That many workers do not think efficiently can easily be confirmed by reference to your own everyday experience. In the service industries, an unthinking approach often alienates customers. In other sectors of industry, expensive and dangerous errors can often be avoided by employees who can deal with tasks which take a non-routine turn. De Bono points out that:

it is very easy to have a general intention to teach thinking as a skill. It is very easy to assume that one has always done this anyway. But when you actually set out to teach thinking directly as a skill it is difficult unless there is something definite to do.

This emphasises the importance of ensuring that the 'something to do' is derived from an accurate notion of what is involved in thinking. As practitioners in vocational education and training, you will find in this book a sound approach to understanding thinking and workable suggestions for translating this understanding into practice in your own occupational area.

While much of the demand for thinking workers has come from employers, learners' interests are also better served by programmes which help them to become thinkers as well as doers. An important claim for academic education is that it develops intellectual abilities of a broad, transferable nature. The evidence that only a few can achieve such skills is fast crumbling, and if there is to be genuine parity between academic and vocational education the teaching of thinking skills must be taken seriously.

OUTLINE OF THE BOOK

Although the book focuses on teaching thinking skills, it is also designed to serve as a basic applied psychology of learning text for vocational teachers and trainers who are seeking teacher/trainer accreditation. Competency-based vocational education implies problem solving in the sense that the objective for the learner is application of knowledge in a range of working situations. This book differs from most 'psychology for teachers' texts in that it starts from a 'core skill' – problem solving – the learning of information being combined with learning to apply it in occupational life. This core skill must be acquired to qualify for GNVQ/GSVQ awards. What is not attempted is the usual 'compare and contrast' tour round cognitive theories but rather an attempt to show how elements of these theories can produce instructional guidelines for vocational tutors. In other words, the focus is on the practical use of cognitive psychology rather than looking at the supporting evidence which can be found in a general psychology text.

Since theories about motivation are explored in most psychology texts and in many books about management, there are no chapters in this book which focus specifically on motivation. There is no universally accepted theory of motivation within psychology. Underlying the ideas in this book is a commitment to research-based cognitive approaches to motivation. Such approaches view people as making choices which are rational in the light of the alternatives they perceive to be available to them. People weigh up the attractiveness of outcomes, the probability of successfully achieving different outcomes and the costs in terms of efforts. The effect on the person's self-esteem from following a particular course of action is an important consideration in appraising alternatives. People will perceive some experiences as potentially damaging to their self-esteem and others as offering a reasonable chance of enhancement. Whether the experiences are likely to be boring or interesting will also be taken into account in making choices, even when the alternatives are limited.

Problem-solving skills are useful in a wide range of social and work activities, and are socially desirable skills which enhance status in many social groups, including those who do not usually conform to mainstream society's norms. Cognitive approaches to motivation would predict that these features of problem-solving skills would help to harness people's efforts towards their development. There are also features of the methods currently being advocated for developing thinking skills which make for more interesting instructional sessions and which reduce the fear of failure which discourages people's efforts to extend their abilities. The creation of a co-operative, non-judgemental learning environment where ideas are explored and developed rather than being pronounced right or wrong is central to teaching thinking skills. Interest is more likely when the instructional focus extends beyond routine tasks. This must happen in learning problem-solving skills which require practice in thinking about, implementing and evaluating solutions to problems. There is sound evidence that people are more interested when a task is just beyond what they can at present understand and do, but not so far in advance of their present capacity that it is not worth trying to crack the problem. A curriculum which is built around problem-solving skills has many features which harness motivation. It provides a richer learning environment in which motivation is not such a big issue as in some traditional programmes.

In Chapter 2 a definition of problem solving and a brief description of its basic intellectual components are introduced and explored through examples of people's unsuccessful attempts to deal with real-life problems. The question of what is meant by intelligence is raised. This chapter also explains how effective learning can be characterised as a form of problem solving.

The role of knowledge in vocational problem solving is considered in Chapter 3. The way that knowledge is learned enhances or inhibits the efficiency of problem solving. Chapter 4 suggests how people can learn information in ways which will enhance its use in subsequent problem solving – in other words, enhance transfer. The point is made that learning to learn information and thinking procedures is central to problem solving. Chapter 5 explains, with many illustrations of problems in vocational and everyday life, how the dual-focus approach to teaching problem solving can be implemented through adaptations and extensions of common instructional techniques. Sections of 'lesson plans' are used in Chapter 6 to emphasise essential differences between the problem-solving approach advocated in the book and conventional instruction. Chapter 7 aims at promoting understanding of the nature of transfer of learning and of the well-documented difficulties people seem to have in transferring learning even when the problems are very similar. There is also consideration of the question of assessing problem solving. This chapter draws extensively on the five Employment Department funded projects which are featured in Thinking and Learning at Work (produced by Blagg and Lewis 1993).

The remaining chapters in the book deal with particular vocational areas. The examples in these chapters are intended for those who have specialised knowledge of the areas. They are an important part of the book because, if the approach is to have credibility, it must contain more than simple applications which are obvious to everybody, and you are asked to select chapters which match your vocational interests. You will usually demand, and rightly so, that theorists spell out not only how an approach works on everyday matters, generally familiar to everyone, but also how it applies to the more technical matters in your particular vocational area. This is a much more difficult demand to meet, for it requires a sound knowledge of a specialist area. That it has been met in Chapters 8, 9 and 10 is due to generous help from vocational tutors working in further and higher education.

The term 'tutor' is used throughout the book to mean anyone who has a role in facilitating the development of others. 'Learner' and 'student' are used interchangeably to refer to those who are being developed both in the workplace and in schools and colleges.

Further reading is suggested at the end of each chapter. Some readings are more suitable for those who wish to pursue theoretical issues in some depth, while others offer learning materials derived from psychological research. The Thinking Skills at Work (TSAW) modules (Blagg *et al.* 1993), discussed in Chapter 7, contain materials for learners which have applications in various employment contexts.

SUMMARY

1

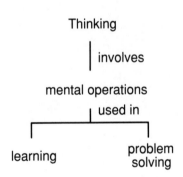

2 Acquiring information offers opportunities to learn also the mental operations involved in learning and problem solving. This book explains how this potential can be realised.

3 The form which thinking operations take is context-dependent.

FURTHER READING

Blagg, N. R. and Lewis, R. E. (eds) (1993) 'Thinking and learning at work', Taunton: Nigel Blagg Associates.

Blagg, N. R., Lewis, R. E. and Ballinger, M. P. (1993) 'Thinking and learning at work', a report on the development and evaluation of the Thinking Skills at Work Modules, Research Series, Moorfoot, Sheffield: The Employment Department.

CBI (1990) 'Towards a skills revolution', reported in 'Thinking and learning at work', N. R. Blagg and R. E. Lewis (eds) Taunton: Nigel Blagg Associates (1993).

de Bono, E. (1974) 'CoRT thinking lessons', Blandford Forum, Dorset: Direct Educational Services.

Entwistle, N. J. (1988) 'Motivational factors in students' approaches to learning', in R. R. Schmeck, (ed.) *Learning Strategies and Learning Styles*, New York: Plenum.

Wolf, A. and Silver, R. (1993) reported in *Thinking and Learning at Work*, N. R. Blagg and R. E. Lewis (eds), Taunton: Nigel Blagg Associates.

Chapter 2

Learning to solve problems and learning as problem solving

It was noted that modern industry requires workers who are capable of applying their knowledge in a flexible, adaptable way and that there is a need to embed the teaching of thinking skills in vocational education and training. It is through thinking more efficiently that we become better problem solvers at work and in our own personal lives.

As noted in Chapter 1, any serious consideration of how to teach problem solving has to start with trying to describe what is involved in efficient thinking. For nearly a century psychologists have been working at understanding thinking. The intention in this chapter is to present only those aspects of psychological theorising which are necessary to create sufficient understanding for you to incorporate the teaching of thinking into your vocational programmes.

Obviously thinking happens inside people's heads. Techniques for direct observation of what is happening inside people's heads when they are thinking have not yet been developed, nor are they likely to be in the foreseeable future. Descriptions of thinking are based on indirect evidence. Various techniques are used which permit inferences to be made about the thinking processes underlying task performance. One technique is the verbal protocol. This is obtained by asking people to describe their thinking by talking aloud as they are completing a problem. Psychologists are particularly interested in charting the thinking of experts in different occupational areas on the assumption that their thinking processes are the most efficient ones for the tasks which they tackle in their working lives.

This chapter begins with a brief consideration of whether it is possible to teach people to think more efficiently. If thinking is manifested in solving problems, it is necessary to have a working definition of 'problem'. Therefore, the chapter goes on to introduce a definition used by psychologists for the purpose of developing descriptions of thinking which can inform the teaching of thinking and problem solving. This definition and a simple but valid description of thinking are explained and illustrated by examples which highlight the main points in a reader-friendly fashion. In the last part of the chapter there is a discussion of the adequacy of the definition offered of a 'problem'. Finally, the notion that efficient learning is an instance of problem solving is discussed.

WHAT ABOUT INTELLIGENCE?

It might be argued that the many entrants to vocational programmes who have poor school achievements are simply not bright enough to learn how to cope with tasks other than the more routine ones. Poor achievement is often interpreted as a reflection of low 'intelligence', in the sense of having poor 'hard wiring', which sets a ceiling on achievement. However, this view of intelligence and the evidence which supported it have been seriously undermined in the last twenty years. There is now good evidence that intelligence in the sense of efficient thinking can be taught. In Japan, for example, the average teenage IQ, which is a frequently cited measure of thinking ability, has been raised to 117 compared with 100 in Britain. 'Although it is not doubted that under some vastly improved system of instruction mental ability may set an upper limit to individual learning attainment, the view that present levels are so constrained is largely discredited' (Simpson 1988).

Activity 2.1 MENSA task one

The task in Figure 2.1 was used by MENSA in its newspaper advertising campaign aimed at recruiting new members. The advertisement informs readers that, if they can solve this problem, they may succeed in achieving a high enough score in an intelligence test to allow them to qualify for membership of MENSA, an association which restricts membership to people whose intelligence scores are at the very top end of the range of scores in the population. You should try to complete this activity within four minutes.

If you cannot complete this task within four minutes you may

Figure 2.1 MENSA task one

It's
as simple
as ABC for
Einstein.
How about
you?

M	E	N	S	A
	A	M	E	
		S		M
	M	E		
		A	M	

Each line, horizontal, vertical and the main diagonals, should contain the letters that make up the word MENSA. If you can fill in all the blank squares you could be eligible to join MENSA, the High IQ Society. Simply fill in the coupon, etc.

wish to look at a list of mental operations at the end of this chapter which are sufficient to achieve a solution. When you have learned these operations and produced a solution, are you more 'intelligent'? The approach in this book is based on the view now shared by many researchers, that 'intelligence' is learnable, in the sense that 'intelligence' consists of a repertoire of concepts and mental operations. Sequences of operations build up into procedures. A Scottish further education lecturer often uses the problem in Figure 2.1 to introduce the idea that mental procedures to deal with problems in an electrical engineering module can be learned. The procedure for the MENSA task is mastered fairly easily even by students who have poor O-level qualifications, and students can learn to transfer it to other relevant tasks.

Activity 2.2 MENSA task two

If you would like to test your grasp of the procedure (at the end of the chapter) for dealing with the MENSA question, you might like to try a second version of the original problem, which has appeared in MENSA advertisements. This version, which requires much the same mental procedure as the first, is in Figure 2.2.

Figure 2.2 MENSA task two

	2		1	3
3		3		1
3	4	3		2
		2	2	
2	3	2	5	2

Each line of 5 numbers must total 14. Place a number into each empty square to solve the puzzle. If you can manage it without a calculator you could be eligible to join MENSA, the High IQ Society. Simply fill in the coupon below for further details and a copy of the self-administered test.

The solution is at the end of this chapter. You might like to try these two problems on friends. Find a friend who needs to be shown the procedure for the first problem, and present the second version without mentioning that the problems require similar mental operations. Research suggests that most people do not transfer a procedure to another relevant problem unless it is pointed out very explicitly that the problems are similar. Try the two problems again with another friend who needs to be shown the procedure for the first problem, but this time tell the friend that the procedure for solving the second problem is similar.

One of the reasons why the teaching thinking movement has not developed as rapidly in this country as in the United States is that certain traditional views of intelligence have been so widely disseminated through the media and in other ways that they are often not questioned by education and training practitioners. This book offers a description, based on current research on learning and thinking, which enables you to understand shortcomings in thinking and problem solving as a temporary stage on a route to further development, and to understand why that development is highly susceptible to instruction. Without such a description it is difficult for you to understand shortcomings other than in terms of irreversible limitations of learners' cognitive equipment. Unless you are provided with a reasonably detailed and accurate description of the mental processes which underlie the problem-solving processes which you are being exhorted to promote, you can hardly be expected to achieve much success in helping learners to think efficiently.

WHAT IS A PROBLEM?

The introduction of 'core skills' into NVQs reflects employers' demands for efficient occupational problem solving and the growing evidence that this competence can be taught. One of these core skills is problem solving, which is thinking in relation to some task whose solution is not immediately obvious to the task performer. Psychologists have been investigating 'problem solving' for most of this century. The essence of definitions in cognitive research is that a problem exists when:

> you want something and do not know immediately what series of mental operations you can use to get it.

In modern societies, problems, as defined above, arise frequently not only in high-level jobs but at all occupational levels. The above description allows a task to be a problem for one person but not for another who has previously encountered that task. Thus the following tasks on page 16 and those on pages 13 and 14 might or might not be a problem depending on the performer's previous experience of the tasks and what he or she has learned (that is, stored efficiently in memory). The following description is taken from a novel where a professor is trying to use a typewriter. This is again consistent with our everyday experience that even people who are regarded as 'intelligent' often have trouble with simple but new tasks.

I'd no idea a typewriter was such a complicated beast. It took a good ten minutes to find the little catch that lets the thing loose. And even when the roller was moving freely, I had enormous difficulty feeding the paper in and winding it up straight.

There is extensive evidence that most people are not good at dealing with tasks they have not previously encountered. For example, try the following tasks.

Activity 2.3 The nine-dot problem

```
•   •   •

•   •   •

•   •   •
```

Draw four straight lines (without raising your pencil from the paper) which will pass through all nine dots.

Activity 2.4 The selection task

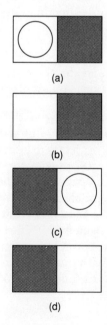

(a)

(b)

(c)

(d)

You are shown a panel of four cards (a), (b), (c) and (d) (see figure) together with the following instructions:

Which of the hidden parts of these cards do you need to see in order to answer the following question decisively?

For these cards is it true that if there is a circle on the left there is a circle on the right? If you cannot produce the answer within ten minutes you should turn to the solution at the end of the chapter.

PROBLEMS WITH PROBLEM SOLVING AT WORK

In the following examples the problems were minor ones, in that the tasks deviated only slightly from their routine versions, but failure to deal with them has significant effects on the organisation's goals. They are presented to illustrate further the definition of 'problem' on page 15 and to introduce a way of describing what is involved in solving problems. They are all reports of real situations reported by vocational trainers and help to explain the current concern with core skills in the NVQ system. The examples are intended to emphasise that problem solving is required at all levels of work and that it has to be learned. There is extensive evidence that the gap between understanding what has to be done in relation to a task and actually doing it is often seriously underestimated. The need for practice in learning practical skills seems to be almost universally recognised, whereas it is often almost overlooked in the case of intellectual skill.

Some illustrations of the definition of 'problem'

1 A new eighteen-year-old typist who had good academic achievements as well as a secretarial qualification was given a handwritten letter to type which was to include the words 'European Social Fund'. As this was referred to frequently in the organisation's correspondence, the writer had abbreviated it to E. . . S. . . F. . .. The letter was presented for signature with European Social Fund typed as it had been written – E. . . S . . . F. . .. The writer of the letter explained that while abbreviations were used to save time they were usually typed in full, and she wrote at the bottom of the letter 'European Social Fund'. The letter was altered and presented again for signature. This time 'European Social Fund' was indeed typed in full – but at the bottom of the

letter with the abbreviated E. . . S. . . F. . . still appearing in the body of the letter.

This example illustrates the essence of current definitions of problem solving which was set out above.

In this example the typist, who was very eager to do well, clearly wanted to produce a mailable letter. Her failure to produce one suggests that she did not know that certain elementary mental operations were necessary, such as generating appropriate questions to herself; for example, during my training, what kind of changes did I have to make? How can I find out what these abbreviations stand for? And later when making the alteration: does this fit in with my previous experience of typing letters?

The task faced by the typist also illustrates the point that the description given of the term 'problem' allows a task to be a problem for one person, but not for another who has previously encountered it. Experienced typists are amused by the error reported above in carrying out what seems to them a trivial task.

2 The next example emphasises this point, that whether a task can be classified as a problem or a routine task depends on the state of knowledge of the problem solver.

Your current wage is £121 a week, which includes a 10 per cent pay rise you have just received. What was your wage before you received this 10 per cent pay rise?

If you were unable to produce the correct answer you will be better able to appreciate why the employees in the remaining examples made errors. You are likely to find the correct answer if you ask yourself the questions, 'Have I come across a similar problem – if so, what procedure did I use? If not, was the previous wage more or less? What percentage of the previous wage is £121? (£121 is 110 per cent of the previous wage.) Can I write out this information in the form of an equation?

$$£121 = \frac{110}{100} \text{ of } £x$$

You may now have converted the problem into a task for which there is a routine procedure. If you do not know this procedure you can look it up in a basic mathematics book.

3 In a coffee bar a customer asked the waitress for black coffee with cold milk. In this coffee bar it was usual to serve coffee

which had been made up with hot milk. The waitress served black coffee with two ice cubes in it but no milk. As in the first example, this waitress seems to have had no awareness that she should have been generating appropriate questions to herself, such as:

Is this request different from the standard order?
What feature is different? (temperature of milk)
What effect on the coffee is the customer trying to achieve? (flavour)
Is cold milk available? (If not) are there alternative ways of achieving the effect wanted by the customer?

By means of questions like these learners manipulate and transform their existing knowledge in order to solve problems. Such questions are described as mental operations. A sequence of mental operations is described as a mental procedure. What has to be learned can therefore be described in terms of mental operations and procedures.

You might be unconvinced that it is necessary to learn to generate questions in order to deal with a task such as the above. Whether you describe a task as routine or as a problem depends on the gap between the mental procedures – namely, sequences of mental operations known by the task performer – and the procedures required for the successful solution of the task. A person can be a good problem solver by learning a large repertoire of mental operations organised into procedures, and by learning to manipulate these when new tasks are encountered. Manipulation involves, for example, combining parts from different sequences of mental operations to generate the new sequences required for a particular task. In the MENSA task, you are combining questions which seek out the parts of the problem which have most information with questions which eliminate one of two pieces of information when a decision has to be made about which bit should fill a particular slot. In the examples you were asked to do on pages 13, 14 and 16, whether or not you produced the correct answer immediately depends on whether you could recall an appropriate series of mental operations. Most adults would immediately produce the answer for the following arithmetic task, whereas many six-year-olds would need to be taught the mental operations listed below:

Jason has 9 sweets and he gives 3 of these sweets away to Andrew. How many sweets does Jason now have? In order to produce the correct answer, young children have to engage in the mental operation of asking themselves whether this is an 'adding' or 'taking away' task and, having classified it as 'taking away', to engage in the mental operations of asking questions such as the following:

Is one number larger than the other? (Yes)

Do I start with the larger or smaller number? (The larger one: 9)

Do I go backwards or forwards from 9? (Backwards)

How many times do I go backwards? (3 times)

What number am I at now? (6)

The manipulation of knowledge to solve this problem is simple, but it is not in its essentials different from many problems tackled in occupational life. Consciousness that mental operations are used in problem solving seems to be one of the necessary conditions for transfer. Interrogation of your own knowledge is a significant component of problem-solving skill, but learning to ask others the right questions is also important. In the following activity, asking questions which yield the maximum relevant information is of great practical significance.

Activity 2.5 A bomb threat

Imagine that you are working in a large organisation and that one day the telephone rings and a voice tells you that a bomb has been placed in your organisation's premises.

List about six questions which would extract the maximum useful information from the caller. Pay particular attention to prioritising the questions, as the caller could ring off at any moment. Check your questions with those at the end of the chapter.

The following are just a few of the mental operations which have been identified by many psychologists as contributing to efficient thinking:

Can you:

1 generate alternative courses of action;

2 identify future consequences of proposed courses of action;

3 describe advantages and disadvantages of courses of action;

4 recall similar problems and actions taken and generalise these to the current problem;

5 find a starting point in a problem which allows you to move forward;
6 check solutions against facts;
7 look for features of a problem which remind you of a problem previously tackled successfully.

As noted earlier, these operations often take the form of questions to yourself; for example, what are the advantages or disadvantages? Can you recall similar problems?

The following activity is intended to raise your awareness of the mental operations you use every day.

Activity 2.6 Questions to solve a work problem

Think of a problem you have encountered at work recently. Which of the above mental operations did you use, if any, in tackling the problem?

Decision making, organising, prioritising and planning are familiar examples of mental procedures. Efficient problem solvers have learned a large number of mental procedures which they can select and recall and adapt with little or no conscious effort, building new procedures by putting together parts of existing ones. Consciousness of the need to search for a procedure is an early signal that a task to be carried out is not a routine one but a problem.

It should be emphasised at this point that there are usually several mental procedures which would produce a solution to any particular problem. It is not implied at any point in this book that there is only one correct procedure. What is being argued is that, if learners do not know any procedures or cannot put together a procedure for a problem, it is in their interest that they should be taught a procedure. This is intended to be a starting point for learners, a first introduction to the possibility that they can learn to construct such procedures for themselves and that, as their repertoire of procedures grows, they will be able to take parts from various procedures and combine them to create new procedures of their own.

It is also important for you to remember that, in teaching problem solving, the emphasis is on teaching mental operations and procedures as well as teaching behaviours. The following example helps to clarify this distinction.

A neighbour has the problem that she has difficulty in starting her elderly car, even although the car has been recently serviced and is in good running order.

You have found that you can start the car first time by adopting the following behaviours which could be taught to your neighbour:

apply maximum choke;
depress clutch fully;
depress accelerator fully and release slowly;
depress accelerator gently and turn ignition key.

Learning these behaviours would not equip the driver with any competence which is transferable to other problems with cars. A problem-solving approach would involve you in thinking about the information this driver needs to understand the problem, teaching the information, and then asking her to suggest some useful questions which would point the way to a solution. If this fails, in your role as tutor you could say, 'I would ask myself what could be done to take some of the load off the engine parts' and then ask the driver to suggest how this could be done.

A word about automatisation of mental procedures

Once people become efficient at using mental operations which are sufficient to deal with various types of task, these sequences of operations fade from their consciousness until they are no longer aware of using them. Psychologists would describe these mental operations as 'automatised' or 'enfolded'.

'Experts' are people who have automatised or enfolded certain mental operations. Automatisation is necessary if you are to deal efficiently with all the tasks which confront you at work and in everyday life. If you had to be conscious of all the sequences of mental operations you use, you could not perform tasks at the speed expected by employers, or at a speed which would enable you to fit in the huge number of things that you expect to be able to do in the course of pursuing a happy and interesting life. On the other hand, this efficiency has a cost – it makes it difficult for you to make your mental operations visible to learners when you are coaching them. If you do not reveal to learners the most efficient operations for a task, they are left to try and discover them for themselves. Learners vary in their ability to discover the most rational sequence of mental operations for a task which is new to them (that is, a problem). A few learners discover most of the appropriate operations while others discover some of the operations, but many discover very few of them. A much larger percentage of school leavers might achieve the entrance qualifications for higher education if thinking processes were taught effectively.

Thus, teaching problem solving involves an instructional approach which targets both the learning of information and its application in solving problems.

If you produced a correct solution on the first trial of the nine-dot problem you have probably automatised or enfolded the appropriate mental operations. If you are not able to produce a correct solution immediately, look at the self-question at the end of the chapter. By generating this question the solution becomes fairly clear.

INTERACTIONS BETWEEN INFORMATION AND MENTAL OPERATIONS

Although the emphasis so far has been on mental operations it was noted in Chapter 1 that efficient problem solving requires both mental operations/procedures and task-relevant information. Problem solving involves an interrogation of the information which you hold in memory or which can be found by using reference books and other resources. The role of information and the importance of how it is stored in memory is discussed in the next chapter. At this point it is useful to think of knowledge as having two aspects.

1 *Information*: all the ideas which you are conscious of knowing. These ideas are often referred to as concepts, which are connected to form propositions (see Chapter 4); e.g., traffic lights give instructions to motorists. These instructions are backed by legal sanctions.
2 *Mental operations* which are built up into *mental procedures*. A question to oneself is an example of a mental operation, and the sequences of questions used would be an example of the operations being built into procedures.
For example, are the traffic lights at green?

If yes: proceed with caution.
If no: are they at red?
If yes: then stop.

You solve problems when you have or can construct adequate information and mental procedures. There is a constant interaction between these two aspects of memory which have been described above as information and procedures. Suppose you wanted to buy a used diesel car. You want to avoid one which has been used as a taxi but are not confident about eliciting an honest answer as to the car's origins. You need a mental procedure which would begin with a self-question such as, what features does a taxi have which are not features of a car in normal use? This question would direct a memory search which might result in retrieval of information such as plates showing taxi licence information. The procedure might continue with, where are they usually fixed? In response to which you might retrieve 'bumpers'. This might lead to your concluding that small holes in the bumper would raise suspicion that the car had been used as a taxi. The interplay between mental procedures and information can be traced in more complex tasks.

Suppose you have a double garage with two doors but no internal partition and you have the problem that you find difficulty in driving the car into the garage without scraping it against the door post. You might start to tackle this problem using the mental operation of generating alternative solutions. Having asked yourself this question about alternatives, you might go into your long-term memory store (see Chapter 3) and come up with:

1 practise driving into tight spaces;
2 remove the two doors and replace with one door.

Another mental operation would be evaluating these solutions by asking yourself about the advantages or disadvantages of each. In order to do this you need to use the mental operation of generating relevant factors. In evaluating the solution of changing the doors you might retrieve from your long-term memory store that cost is a factor. In order to use the mental operation of evaluating the cost, you need to generate components of cost. Until you can produce the information to answer this question, you cannot proceed further in solving the problem.

You might retrieve from memory the information that components of cost would include removal of the two single doors and the cost of a new double door. However, if you did not also retrieve or find out information about other components of cost such as insertion of a supporting beam, your answer to the 'evaluating the cost' question and the eventual solution would be flawed.

Try the following activity. Its purpose is to illustrate further the relationship discussed above between mental operations and task relevant information.

Activity 2.7 The thinking DIY

Suppose you want to put up book shelves, approximately 6 feet tall by 8 feet wide, in your lounge.

1 Write questions which you might ask yourself as part of the planning for this task.
2 Find someone who is a trained carpenter or an experienced DIY enthusiast and ask him or her to generate appropriate questions for this task.
3 Compare your list of questions with those of the more expert person in (2) above.

(If you do not have a DIY friend, you will find an 'expert' list at the end of this chapter.)

You will have noticed that the questions you ask yourself are dependent to some extent on the information you have stored in memory, while, as already noted, some questions are useful in almost every situation. For example, 'Have I come across a problem like this before? How does this problem differ from previous similar ones? Are those differences significant?' Others are quite specific to the task and depend on subject knowledge. The joiner will ask more questions about the task in Activity 2.7 than the beginner at DIY. The joiner's questions will be based on information about woods, fixing materials and so on. If you do not know that different types of wood are more likely to bend or less likely to bend under the weight of books, you cannot generate the question 'What type of wood will hold up under the weight of the books?' Without expert information you cannot generate some questions, let alone answer them. In order to be effective, your knowledge of a subject must be linked to your knowledge of how to apply the subject.

Clearly, this view of the content of human memory has some

resemblance to descriptions of how computers work. Artificial Intelligence has had a very strong influence on theorising about thinking and its manifestation in problem solving. One useful way of describing the relationship between Artificial Intelligence and theories of problem solving is to say that Artificial Intelligence is a metaphor for thinking about thinking.

HOW ADEQUATE IS THE DEFINITION OF A PROBLEM?

Definitions in psychology are rarely totally adequate. For example, the validity of definitions of intelligence produced by psychologists have been hotly debated both within the profession and outside it. This is not surprising when you are trying to capture something as complex as an aspect of mind. Some people might say that many of the tasks described in this chapter are not problems but simply an inability to apply knowledge correctly. Psychologists would not disagree that problem solving is application of relevant knowledge to a task, but research suggests that this application is far from being a simple matter. Many researchers have found that there is a huge discrepancy between students' scores on tests which measure their ability to give explanations of what they have learned and their scores on tests designed to measure application of that same knowledge to tasks which are even slightly different from a familiar version.

In a wide range of subject matter and professions – mathematics, applied sciences, nursing, town planning – substantially lower scores have been reported on 'application' tasks. Employers also confirm the scarcity of this ability to apply knowledge effectively.

If all task performance involves the application of relevant knowledge, it is difficult to argue that some instances of knowledge application are to count as 'problems' and others are to be excluded, other than on the basis that the performer can or cannot produce a solution. The complexity of the knowledge itself and of the mental procedures required for its selection and application vary from one task to another. What is common to all tasks is that appropriate knowledge has to be selected, a mental procedure for its application has to be selected or constructed, and the performer has to monitor his or her execution of that procedure. If all task performance depends on these intellectual processes, it is difficult to argue that some tasks which people cannot immediately do correctly are 'problems' and some are not.

Although it is not disputed that some tasks are more difficult than others for some people or that some tasks can be mastered more quickly than others by some learners, it is more logical and useful to conceive of tasks lying along a continuum of complexity. The definition of 'problem' on page 15 was developed by cognitive psychologists for the purpose of identifying mental processes which are involved in problem solving, their reasoning being that identifying what has to be learned might lead to more effective instructional programmes. If a person is unable to orchestrate the appropriate procedure for a given task it can be described as a problem and you can proceed to identify which mental steps and which aspects of knowledge the person needs to learn to produce a solution.

Consideration of the concept of problem could be the focus of entire academic texts. The purpose of this chapter is to suggest a valid way of conceptualising a problem for the purpose of improving instruction.

LEARNING IS PROBLEM SOLVING: THE RELATIONSHIP BETWEEN LEARNING AND PROBLEM SOLVING

Problem-solving skills are thinking skills. Learning and study skills are also thinking skills. Learners have to use certain mental operations and procedures to store new information in a way which enables them to retrieve it easily when it is required. People can become good learners in the same way as they can become good problem solvers. Many of the mental operations which are useful in problem solving are also useful in learning. For example, when confronted with a problem, it is useful to search one's memory for a similar task and its solution. The same mental operation would be efficient when something new has to be learned. Thus, if you were learning about investment trusts as a savings vehicle, you might identify unit trusts as a similar vehicle and then go on to use the mental operations of identifying the similarities and differences in dealing with these two types of saving plans. An important point is that the memory search would be most efficient if you had previously stored the information about unit trusts under the category 'types of investments' and you had identified investment trusts as belonging to this same category – that is, matching the task to the correct category. Memory search for something similar would be efficient because you would be able to start it with a category name, 'investments', thereby confining the search to a very small area of memory. The same point applies to many of the mental procedures used in problem solving. For example, when you ask yourself about relevant factors, consequences of actions, advantages and disadvantages of doing this rather than that, you are searching for a particular category of information in your memory. If the information has been entered into memory under an appropriate category heading it will be easier to retrieve.

All the items which belong to a particular category do not impinge on you at the same time, but rather over a period which may extend to several decades. If you do not categorise information, it is entered haphazardly in memory and is therefore difficult to retrieve when required for problem solving. Therefore learning and problem solving are interdependent mental activities. Efficient problem solving depends on relevant information having been entered initially in memory in an appropriate category. Efficient learning depends on using many of the mental procedures which are used in problem solving to sort out incoming information. If it is to be efficient, learning should be a problem-solving process. Therefore, in teaching problem solving, you are also teaching people how to learn for themselves.

Many vocational tutors have reported deficits in learning skills which lead to poor problem solving. After watching a demonstration of how to make peppercorn sauce, the selection of peppercorns from an ingredients store was a problem for most of the learners. They were found trying to grind currants for this sauce! This suggests that during the demonstration they were not asking themselves about the features which distinguish peppercorns from currants – namely, that peppercorns are hard, smooth and spherical, while currants have none of these features. The features of currants would rule out grinding as a procedure. Tutors blamed themselves for not labelling all the items in a storeroom, even though they know this would not be done in the workplace. A better solution would be to teach the learners the mental process of identifying features which enable them to select the correct ingredients. Many instances of poor problem solving have their source in poor learning of information and mental procedures.

SUMMARY

1 The essence of definitions in cognitive research is that a problem exists when:

   you want something and do not know immediately what series of mental operations you can use to get it.

2 Inability to find an acceptable solution is not an indication that someone is simply not very 'bright'. It is an indication that that person needs to be taught appropriate sequences of mental operations.

3 Mental operations often take the form of questions to oneself and answers from oneself.

4 A sequence of mental operations can be described as a mental procedure.

5 When a sequence of mental operations has been well learned, the operations fade from consciousness – they become automatised or enfolded.

6 Efficient learning is a problem-solving task.

MENTAL PROCEDURES FOR DEALING WITH THE PROBLEMS IN CHAPTER 2

Activity 2.1   MENSA task one

	6	7	8	9	10
1	M	E	N	S	A
2		A	M	E	
3			S		M
4		M	E		
5			A	M	

The following is one mental procedure (but not the only one) which will enable you to produce a solution.

First, number the lines in the puzzle as shown above to enable you to follow the procedure. The procedure consists of asking yourself the following questions:

1 What am I required to do?
2 What line has only one unknown and which letter is it? (Enter this letter in the diagram.)
3 Which horizontal line has two unknowns and which letters are unknown?
4 Which lines must fit with line 2?
5 Which letter is used already in one of these lines? (Enter the unused letter; enter the letter left in the remaining line.)
6 Which two letters are missing from the diagonal line MAS and which lines must fit with this diagonal line.
7 Which of these letters is used already in one of these 'fitting' lines? (Enter the unused letter; enter the letter left in the remaining line.)
8 Do any lines have just one missing letter? (Enter this letter.)
9 Repeat step (viii) until the puzzle is complete.

Your chart should now look as follows:

M	E	N	S	A
S	A	M	E	N
E	N	S	A	M
A	M	E	N	S
N	S	A	M	E

Activity 2.3 The nine-dot problem

You should ask the question, 'Can the line extend beyond the dot framework?'

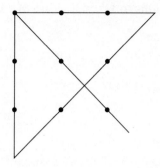

Activity 2.4 Solution to the selection task

The solution is cards (a) and (d) because only a circle on the left without a circle on the right allows a negative answer to the question. (c) is superfluous because, although it could allow an affirmative answer, it could not allow a negative answer; hence it is useless.

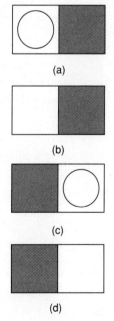

The selection task (Psychology Exhibition, Science Museum, 1977)

Activity 2.5 Questions to ask in the case of a bomb threat

1 When will it go off?
2 Where is it?
3 What does it look like?
4 Why are you doing this?
5 Who are you?
6 Where are you?

Activity 2.7 Putting up bookshelves: suggested self-questions

What quality of finish do I want? What are the other finishes in
the room?
Would hardwood, softwood or composite boarding offer the
finish wanted? Which of these also meets cost constraints?
What kind of wall is it? (e.g., brick, stud partition); therefore what
kind of fixing should be used?
What type of bracketing is available for support? Does the
bracketing chosen require a timber plate for fixing?
How many brackets do I need to prevent sagging – what is the
weight of the books? – how firm is the shelf material?
How do I keep the shelves level?
What tools do I require?
What kind of nails, screws, etc. are needed?
Can I handle the shelving material without help?
Do the ends of the shelves need to be dressed?

FURTHER READING

Blagg, N. (1991) *'Can we teach intelligence?' – a comprehensive evaluation of
Feuerstein's Instrumental Enrichment Programme*, NJ: Lawrence Erlbaum.
Eysenck, H and Kamin, L. (1981) *Intelligence: The Battle for the Mind*,
London: Macmillan.
Howe, M.J.A.(1989) 'Separate skills or general intelligence: the autonomy
of human abilities', *British Journal of Educational Psychology* 59 (3).
Richardson, K. (1991) 'Reasoning with Raven – in and out of context',
British Journal of Educational Psychology 16 (2): 129–38.
Simpson, M. (1988) 'Improving learning in schools – what do we know? A
cognitive science perspective', *Scottish Educational Review* 20 (1): 22–31.
Tuma, D.T. and Reif, F.R. (eds) (1980) *Problem Solving and Education*,
Hillsdale, NJ: Lawrence Erlbaum.

Chapter 3

Information matters in learning and problem solving

Many books and courses in problem solving avoid discussing how the vast quantity of information in human memory is brought to bear on vocational and everyday problems. Although this is a complex matter it is necessary to confront it, if the approach to teaching problem solving is to work.

In Chapter 2, mental operations and procedures were described as efficient tools both for interrogating one's existing knowledge in order to solve problems and for learning new information – that is, storing it in memory in such a way that it can be retrieved easily and applied when problems arise. There is sound evidence that the way in which information is learned (namely, stored in memory) inhibits or enhances problem solving. You will apply the mental procedures required in problem solving most effectively when you learn the information in an organised way.

Obviously, there is no point in using mental procedures to interrogate your knowledge if it is stored so haphazardly in the first place that you can't find the knowledge required, or at least enough of it to make it feasible to locate the shortfall in some text or disk. Inefficient information storage seems to be one of the reasons why many people are poor problem solvers. The mental operations and procedures which make up a problem-solving approach are also efficient for learning new information. By using these procedures you are likely to improve your organisation of knowledge, thereby making it more accessible.

When you find that you can access your knowledge more easily, you will become more motivated to persist with a problem-solving approach to your work. So important is the (occupational) knowledge base that some psychologists would go so far as to say that, if it is taught properly, problem solving will almost take care of itself. However, it is generally agreed that, like scissors, an effective approach to problem solving needs two blades which work together – information and procedures. If you are to teach problem-solving skills you need to consider how to improve your teaching of both the information base and procedures.

In this chapter and the next one, the focus is on helping learners to develop mental operations/procedures which are efficient for acquiring information and organising it in memory in ways which make it easily retrievable when it is required for application to problems. The focus in the next chapter shifts to helping learners to develop mental operations and procedures which are efficient for applying their information in order to solve problems. The approach suggested in this book is applicable both to learning information and to applying it to solve problems.

At the heart of the approach, which is well founded in theory and research, is the notion that any instructional activity can, and should, have a dual focus. Firstly, it must, of course contribute to achievement of the targeted competence, which includes information underlying 'practical' tasks. However, what is mostly neglected is the second focus, which is the development of the thinking skills which are inextricably linked with the competency. This extra yield on instructional activity can be realised by most people after a two- to three-day course during which you can extend your existing techniques in fairly straightforward ways which are described and illustrated in this chapter and in Chapter 4.

These thinking skills might include identifying features which enable you to recognise something as an instance of a particular category and to use this categorisation to guide your behaviour. For example, if you are buying salmon steaks for a restaurant there are features you can learn to notice (soft, greyish, oily or watery) which allow you to categorise the salmon as not fresh and therefore to avoid a bad buy. This thinking skill of looking for important features can be transferred to many learning and problem-solving tasks; for example, in helping frail, elderly people to select accommodation, you can look for features such as the number of steps from pavement to door. Examples of features which are important in hotel catering include storage space, the required profit margins and known preferences of guests.

This dual focus approach means that not only the execution of a task has to be taught – such as drawing up simple trading, profit and loss accounts and a balance sheet. What is equally important is the development of thinking skills such as how to decide which of the accounting categories (expenditure, revenue, asset or liability) can be used to record insurance paid in advance. The opportunity to develop thinking skills is lost if there is only one focus to the instruction – correct task completion.

It follows from the basic idea that thinking activities are an integral part of efficient performance of all tasks, that the teaching approach is an embedded one, rather than one which takes the form of separate, add-on courses in thinking. This means that you do not teach thinking skills in general, but those skills which enhance performance of the task in hand, whether it is learning to construct a sentence in Spanish or putting up shelves. It is a customised approach.

It is useful to highlight six propositions which summarise the approach and which will be referred to throughout the book.

1 For most complex vocational tasks, including mastery of the underlying information, it is possible for experts to specify sequences of mental operations which build up into mental procedures which are necessary and sufficient to complete these tasks.

2 These operations/procedures need to be made as visible as possible to learners.

3 The teaching strategy should be such that learners are enabled not only to store and apply the mental operations/procedures but also to generate new sequences of mental operations when required. This is the cognitive basis of thinking which is variously described as flexible, adaptable, lateral, creative, etc. – or, as in this book, problem solving.

4 Learning of mental operations is at its most effective and most transferable when learners are consciously noting that the operations are being learned and they are encouraged to use them in a variety of learning and problem-solving tasks.

5 Regular and systematic practice in using the thinking procedures is necessary. To encourage transfer, learners should practise thinking on tasks both within their vocational area and in another area.

6 Practice should be followed by feedback dialogues in which the thinking procedure used by the learners is explored.

WHAT IS MEANT BY ORGANISING INFORMATION IN MEMORY?

In order to understand what is meant by organisation of knowledge and its crucial importance in learning and problem solving, it is necessary to give a brief account of what psychologists know about efficient ways of storing knowledge in memory. The experiences you have in operating in and on the world bring you information, some of which you store for future use. These experiences occur both inside and outside educational institutions. The word 'experience' is used in the widest sense to mean reading/listening/thinking/performing various skills/ carrying out procedures/coping with interpersonal relationships and with emotions like love, hate and so on. In bringing up children and in participating in various relationships at home and at work you learn what pleases or upsets others, and you use this information to head off conflict, to secure co-operation in carrying out tasks and in general to smooth interpersonal relationships. Watching others coping with tasks also brings you information. 'Observational learning' (Bandura 1977) sets out one of the more important theories about how you acquire new information. Put very simply, this theory says that you notice the main features or principles underlying other people's performance. You are particularly likely to store the features if the way of dealing with a task or situation appears to have for you what Bandura calls 'functional value', meaning that you can see the benefits it may bring you. When you hear politicians being asked awkward questions during an interview, you may notice that the main principle they use is to provide an answer but not one which addresses the question posed. For many of you, this principle could be applied to your advantage in many situations. This information has to be stored in some form inside your head. It would be uneconomical and inefficient for you to take a kind of verbal or visual photograph of every experience, preserving every detail of it. Human societies avoid this clutter by developing a language, which provides a way of summarising the detailed information of an experience.

Psychologists refer to the words of language as 'concepts' – the tools for labelling ideas. The word 'concept' is used to describe all words in a language – not just certain kinds of words. One example can be found in early childhood where children struggle to achieve understanding of concepts like 'behind', 'above' and 'beside'. If you have very young children, you could check their understanding of these concepts by asking them to place a toy behind or beside something.

In all vocational and professional areas a system of concepts is built up which has special meaning within the occupation – for example, a white sauce, a balance sheet, a report or a deadlight window. If these concepts help to describe things more precisely than they could be described with ordinary everyday concepts they are not merely 'jargon'. You have just been introduced to the concepts of 'mental procedure' and 'mental operation'. If you look back to the explanation of their meaning you will see the summarising advantage of concepts – they can save you using a large number of other words and they allow you to communicate more precisely.

Just as locating a file relies on all the files being arranged according to some principle – for instance, a sales office may arrange its files first of all into geographical areas if it has customers

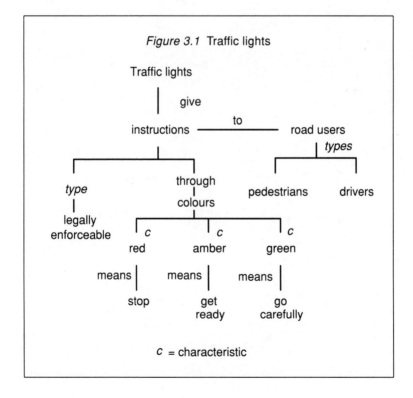

Figure 3.1 Traffic lights

spread all over the country and then arrange them alphabetically within each area – retrieving knowledge from memory depends on the concepts being arranged according to a system which suits the needs of the user. An efficient system for organising knowledge in human memory is based on meaning, in that concepts which are meaningfully related to one another are stored together. This suits humans because they usually want to retrieve pieces of knowledge which together make sense rather than random strings of words and numbers. It is much more likely that you would want to recall the plot in a novel than that you would want to recall its ISBN; for example, 0–335–15325–9.

The results of many experiments suggest that concepts which are meaningfully related to one another are stored in a structure which shows the relationships between the concepts in that structure. Figures 3.1–3.5 show some examples of concept structures.

Words which are commonly used in prose to describe relationships between ideas are in italics in Figures 3.1–6.8; being aware of

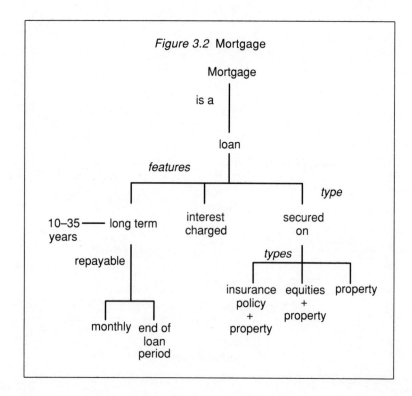

Figure 3.2 Mortgage

frequently occurring relationships helps you to assimilate prose. From these examples of concept structures you can see that the meaning of any concept is derived from its relationship with others. Put simply, the meaning of a concept is made up of a number of features which could be described as sub-concepts. For example, the main feature of traffic lights is that they give instructions of a certain type and by particular means. The next example shows how the concept 'mortgage' may be represented in memory by the structure in Figure 3.2.

In psychological terms, what is meant by understanding information is that the relevant concepts have been connected, as in Figures 3.1–3.6.

Understanding is not an all-or-nothing matter. Rather, it develops as more relevant information is received and connected to an existing concept structure. Depth of understanding could be described as the number of meaningful links with other concepts.

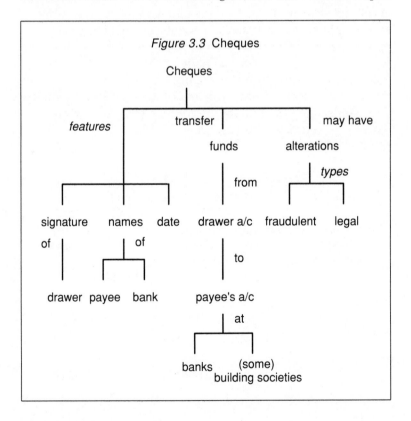

Figure 3.3 Cheques

A chemistry teacher reported that after completing a PhD in chemistry, she realised that when she finished her first degree she had very limited understanding of chemistry in the sense of having made links between the concepts which make up this subject area. It is very common to hear teachers say that they have a better grasp of their subject after they have taught it for a few years. This happens because effective teaching depends on tutors having identified relations between important concepts in their subject. Teaching also makes us more aware of the fact that the same pattern of relationships recurs in different subject matter. In the example of the pattern in Figure 3.1 (Traffic lights), the pattern is one of something or someone transmitting information of a certain type, by a certain means, to specific others. A similar pattern is found in many other concepts (such as a will, conditions of service). The pattern of relationships in Figure 3.3 (Cheques) is mainly one of features, types and function, and would be repeated in concept structures which give meaning to invoices, statements and other financial documents. Becoming aware of these patterns makes it easier to learn new concepts, because you can simply recall the familiar structure and fill in the blank 'slots'.

Of course the structures in Figures 3.1–3.6 show only a tiny fraction of the knowledge you may have stored in memory. Thousands or even millions of concept structures would be required to represent the vast amount of knowledge you store

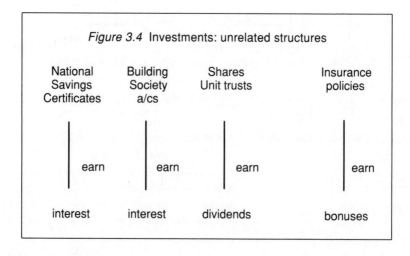

Figure 3.4 Investments: unrelated structures

National Savings Certificates	Building Society a/cs	Shares Unit trusts	Insurance policies
earn	earn	earn	earn
interest	interest	dividends	bonuses

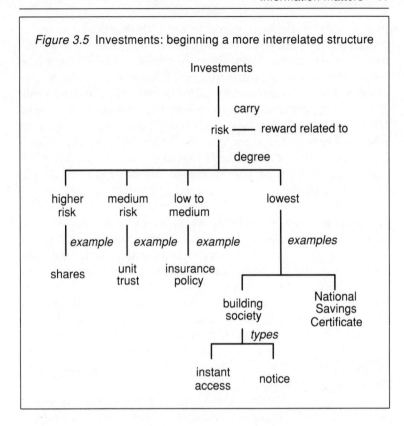

Figure 3.5 Investments: beginning a more interrelated structure

in memory, and there would be many links between concept structures. The structures themselves change as you gain more knowledge. Your knowledge of investments may build up gradually and you may for some time have separate concept structures, as in Figure 3.4.

Later these separate structures may combine into one better-organised structure, such as Figure 3.5.

PROBLEM SOLVING REQUIRES LARGER, MORE LINKED CONCEPT STRUCTURES

An important difference between experts and novices in any occupational area is that the experts store their knowledge in larger concept structures and have created more links between the structures. These larger structures and the links between them enable knowledge to be retrieved more easily. Instead of the pieces of information required to solve the particular types of problems being scattered in a haphazard way across many relatively unrelated structures, they are stored either within a few large structures or in structures which have many links to one another. Larger structures are likely to be created around more general concepts or principles rather than around very specific facts. For example, in Figure 3.5 the general principle around which a larger structure about investment vehicles can be created is that the degree of reward is related to the degree of risk.

In a psychology of ageing course the development of the learners' knowledge was measured at various points on the course. A characteristic of learners who were most successful at applying their knowledge to problems was the increase they showed in various aspects of knowledge organisation. It was found that they made more use of categorising and sub-categorising the concepts into structures. These learners had similar entrance qualifications, but as the course progressed the most successful learners showed marked changes towards the larger, well-integrated structures described on page 41. The learners who were eventually average in knowledge application – namely, problem solving – showed less of a change. Shown below in Figure 3.6 is an example of categorising and sub-categorising information.

Those who were poor at knowledge application showed either no change or a decrease in measures of knowledge organisation throughout the course. These results suggest that inappropriate development of overall relations of concepts impedes the application of knowledge to problems and that systematic provision for knowledge organisation needs to be built into the programme. This would seem to be particularly important in a modularised system.

Another example of storing information around a more general principle comes from a study which found that competent technicians in electronics reconstructed drawings of circuit diagrams according to the function of the elements in the circuit (amplifiers, rectifiers, filters), whereas novices produced chunks based on proximity of the elements to one another. In another study, novices differed from experts when categorising physics problems in that the experts categorised according to physics principles, whereas novices used superficial features of the problems or what they thought were important key words.

Experts' vocational knowledge is broader than that of poorer

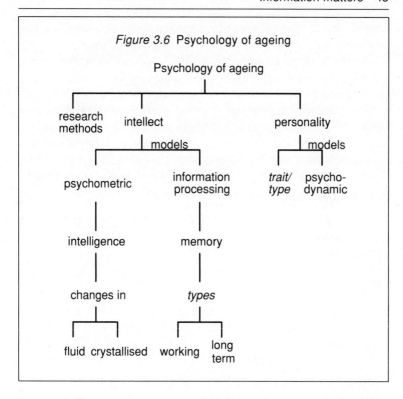

Figure 3.6 Psychology of ageing

performers. This suggests that teaching the absolute minimum knowledge to carry out a task may impede problem solving. It would pay off in the long run to spend a little time in ensuring that learners understand how each set of information fits in to a larger framework of knowledge. For example, in working through the first three SCOTVEC (Scottish Vocational Education Council) modules in Financial Record Keeping, many learners do not understand how the financial information which they record in different ways fits together to form a larger accounting picture which provides the basis for senior management decisions. It is not difficult to teach beginners how the total figures they are recording for sales, purchases, stock, expenses of various kinds, debtors and creditors fit together to yield information which contributes to these decisions.

In almost all studies of problem solving in occupational areas, good problem solvers had a better understanding of the broad principles of subjects. It is interesting that at present one of the core skills in Japanese vocational education is described as 'the fundamental scientific principles which do not change'.

A related aspect of expert knowledge is that their vocational knowledge is well tied into their overall world knowledge. In one experiment, transfer of what had been learned in binomial probability problems depended on whether the learners had been helped to connect probability theory to their real-world knowledge. A group who had begun their learning in terms of their experience with batting averages or probability of rain could tackle a wider range of new problems than groups whose learning was restricted to the components of the formula and how to apply the formula to examples.

SUMMARY

Good problem solvers:

1 organise their information into categories (concept structures) and know the relationships between different categories – this helps them to retrieve all relevant information quickly when they are solving problems;
2 reorganise their concept structures as they acquire more information;
3 understand the fundamental principles in their subject.

FURTHER READING

The additional reading suggested is relevant also to later chapters.

Bandura, A. (1977) *Social Learning Theory,* Englewood Cliffs, NJ: Prentice-Hall.

Gagné, R.M. and Dick, W. (1983) 'Instructional psychology', *Annual Review of Psychology* 34: 261–95.

Gagné, R.M. and Smith, E.C. (1962) 'A study of the effects of verbalisation on problem solving', *Journal of Experimental Psychology* 63: 12–18.

Glaser, R., (1984) 'Education and thinking: the role of knowledge', *American Psychologist* 39: 93–104.

Howard, R. W. (1987) *Concepts and Schemata,* London: Cassell.

Landa, L. (1976) in *Instructional regulation and control*, Englewood Cliffs, NJ: Educational Technology Publications, 1976.

Soden, R. (1993) 'Teaching thinking skills in vocational education', Technical Report No. 13, Employment Dept, Research and Development Series, Moorfoot, Sheffield.

Chapter 4

Learning to learn for problem solving

SEQUENCING INFORMATION IN CERTAIN WAYS

If how you store information crucially influences your problem solving, you need to think about instructional practices likely to cause efficient knowledge organisation. The notion of epitomising is very useful. To epitomise is to provide an overview which is not a preview of all the important course content, but, rather, instruction in a few fundamental and representative ideas and the major relationships among these ideas, thus conveying the essence of the entire content. An illustration of an attempt to epitomise the (cognitive) academic literature on problem solving uses the fundamental ideas of mental procedures and information structures and the relationship between these ideas. The structure of this book also illustrates epitomising, in that Chapter 2 introduces the essence of the book, with more detailed consideration of the ideas appearing in subsequent chapters. A preview of content appears towards the end of Chapter 1 under 'outline of book'. Notice how this differs from the epitomising of Chapter 2, which introduces all the important ideas that are developed in the later chapters. The learning materials in Chapter 10 for double entry bookkeeping also represent an attempt to translate these notions into instructional plans. Advertisements created by leading agencies are also good examples of capturing essence, as are some cartoons.

Figure 3.5 (see page 41) is an example of an epitomiser for an introductory module on personal investment, as it captures the main concept of degree of risk being related to expected reward. Figure 3.4 (page 40) is not an example of epitomising, because it does not contain the more general concepts – investment and degree of risk – which are essential for understanding this area. Rather, it begins with the less general concepts in this area, which are the names of the different investment vehicles and their features. This is not to say that these vehicles should not be first introduced by their different names, some of which will be familiar to learners. The point is that, at the first meeting, the names of the products should then be related to the more general concepts of the risk/reward relationship in investing, the more specific features of interest, bonuses and capital gains being considered at later meetings. Figure 4.1 shows a possible epitomiser for a discussion of loans. Notice that it does not start with specific information about, say, overdrafts. The epitomiser is essentially a wide-angle shot.

Working out epitomisers for your own area is surprisingly difficult at first, but it is a competence well worth practising since it requires you to clarify the essence of any area of knowledge. Such clarification is enormously helpful to learners whose main difficulty is separating the wood from the trees.

Epitomising always entails identifying the more general but not necessarily more abstract ideas – for example, animal is not more abstract than polar bear but it is more general. In providing information for visitors about the Glasgow underground system, the more general proposition which could make up an epitomiser is that there is an inside and outside circle. An important point is

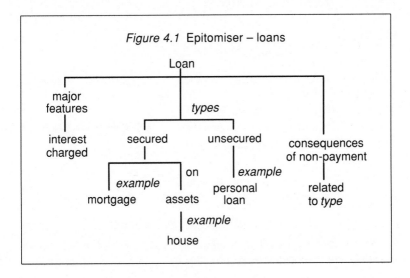

Figure 4.1 Epitomiser – loans

that more general – sometimes called superordinate – concepts are not necessarily more difficult to learn. The instructional sequence begins with this special kind of overview which contains very little detail. (Chapter 2 is very long for an epitomiser, but it is divided into sections which would not all be presented in one 'lesson'.) The next step in the sequence is to add a certain amount of complexity or detail in one aspect of the overview, after which the overview is reviewed and the ideas presented earlier are pointed out. In Figure 3.5, after the epitomiser has been discussed, the specific features of any one of the savings vehicles could be considered in detail, but the discussion should finish by relating the vehicle back to the risk/reward concepts. This level of detail is continued until a desired level of complexity has been reached on all to-be-learned aspects of the subject matter. A central idea in this theory is periodically interrelating the individual ideas by discussing how they fit within a larger picture.

Another example of an epitomiser appears in Figure 4.2, which tries to highlight the fundamental questions which run through theories about personality. Many learners in courses such as personnel management which draw on psychological theories find it difficult to cope with the fact that there are often many theories about one aspect of human behaviour – for instance, personality or motivation. An epitomiser such as the one in Figure 4.2 helps learners to deal with the complexity of the information by pointing out common threads.

Figure 4.2   Personality theories

The following is a framework to which you can attach your ideas as they develop.
In any area of study you should ask:

WHAT ARE THE CENTRAL QUESTIONS?

In the study of social behaviour – or 'personality' – a central question is:

to what extent can people *change*?

and

how does the change come about?

There are 'sub-questions' within this question; some of the important ones could be:

1 Are there individual differences in biological make-up and to what extent might these differences set limits to change? (For example, differences in central nervous system functioning, etc.)

2 Does early childhood experience exert a disproportionate influence on adult behaviour? Might certain childhood experiences make it difficult to change in adult life?

3 To what extent is 'personality' learned – and therefore to what extent can society 'make' and 're-make' the person?

4 What can be learned that facilitates 'personality' changes? (e.g., social role behaviour? self-knowledge?)

WHY DO THESE QUESTIONS MATTER?

Answers to these questions can inform social policy – and also be used to justify policies – such as provision of pre-school care and education; fostering and adoption of older children; regimes in prisons.

Activity 4.1 Constructing an epitomiser

Epitomising: select one 'module' (30–40 hours of contact) which is of interest to you.

Try to construct an epitomiser for this module; that is, work out the most fundamental ideas which run through the module and other modules in the same vocational area. In other words, find out the essence of this vocational area.

HELPING LEARNERS TO FIT TO-BE-LEARNED CONCEPTS INTO THEIR EXISTING CONCEPT STRUCTURES

In general, there is a high degree of consensus among researchers that systematic attention needs to be given to helping learners to establish connections not only between concepts they are learning, but also between these concepts and their other world knowledge. Learners must develop in memory concept structures rather than isolated concepts. Some researchers have shown that learners do not understand the everyday reality behind symbols and concepts used in subjects such as maths and accounting. Therefore it is worth trying to ensure that the concept structures which learners develop include the relationships between new concepts and those they know already. Beginning students in accounting often have difficulty when they are asked to apportion (share out) among departments, in some sensible way, overheads such as heating, advertising and first aid. They apparently fail to relate this problem to their real-world information, that the cost of heating is more affected by the floor space a department occupies than by the number of people working in the department. If they did join together relevant pieces of information, they could easily see that the proportion of the total heating cost to be charged to each department would be the proportion of the total floor space it occupies.

As the instruction proceeds, of central importance is the regular use of learning experiences which push learners into successive reorganisations of their developing knowledge structures into larger units that contain all the concepts and procedures needed for major types of problems in their occupational area. The materials in Chapter 10 illustrate how this was done in learning materials for double-entry bookkeeping.

The instructional implication of this, if the learner is to build up concept structures which enhance problem solving, is that you must tackle several crucial tasks.

HELPING LEARNERS TO UNDERSTAND HOW INFORMATION CAN BE STORED EFFICIENTLY

Learning to store information is, of course, an enhancement of learning.

There are suggested activities for developing learners' insights into efficient information sorting and storing on pages 51–61.

You should also help learners to apply their insights into efficient information processing by frequent reminders *that they should be questioning themselves about*:

1 *what they know already which is related to the to-be-learned information*. You can model this questioning by saying aloud, which document/theory/principle/process have I come across which is similar to this one?
2 *relationships between concepts*. Some relationships between concepts are of the 'this causes (or may cause) that' type, e.g., slugs cause damage to certain plants. Some relationships are of the

type 'this is evidence of that', e.g., a sign of the presence of slugs is a silvery trail in a garden path.

3 *the main features of concepts or procedures.* The main features of a TESSA savings account are that the interest is tax-free and that savings are limited to a total of £9,000 per person over five years;

4 *how to-be-learned information might be categorised.* Many procedures have steps which can be categorised into planning, implementing, monitoring, evaluating.

You can model these learning enhancement questions by posing them and inviting learner contributions. If it is not appropriate to use questioning during the presentation (for instance, because the group is very large), much of the benefit can still be derived by suggesting connections with learners' existing knowledge and by highlighting features, relationships between concepts and possible categories. It should be made clear to the learners that you are trying to kick-start their own self-questioning.

It is of the utmost importance that you act on the fundamental principle that each instructional encounter offers the potential for you not only to put across information, but also to do something to draw the learners' attention to the points set out above. In dealing with these points about how knowledge is made up, you are demonstrating how to learn efficiently.

The tasks described are all directed at helping the learner to use the mental operations which make learning efficient. The following activities are also useful in helping learners to gain insight into these mental operations.

Activity 4.2 Categorising to learn

This activity is intended to demonstrate to learners that categorisation of information enhances learning and remembering.

Procedure

1 Explain to the group that they will be given a brief learning task. Ask them to do their best on it, so they can see a learning principle at work.

2 Give out list A to every second person in the group. Give out list B to the remaining people in the group.

3 Ask everyone to turn the lists over and study for 60 seconds.

4 At the end of 60 seconds ask everyone to turn the lists face down
   and write as many words as they can remember on the data
   sheet. Give them about three minutes to do this.
5 Ask everyone to check their own work .
6 Appoint a person in each group to find the mean. Each member
   of the group passes their own number of correct words to this
   person. Those who studied list A, which was organised in
   categories, should achieve a higher mean score than those who
   did list B, in which the words appeared unclassified.

Discussion

1 What is the difference between the two lists? You should show
   the two lists together on an overhead projector.
2 Why is there a difference in performance between the two lists?
3 Ask the people who had list B if they tried to impose some kind
   of categorisation on this list.
4 A classified list is helpful only if you understand the main
   categories. Can you think of areas of knowledge where the
   concepts used to categorise are unfamiliar to you?

List A

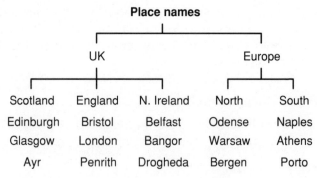

	Place names	
UK		Europe

Scotland	England	N. Ireland	North	South
Edinburgh	Bristol	Belfast	Odense	Naples
Glasgow	London	Bangor	Warsaw	Athens
Ayr	Penrith	Drogheda	Bergen	Porto

List B

Edinburgh
Naples
Bergen
United Kingdom
Glasgow

England
Athens
North
Ayr
Porto
London
South
Warsaw
Penrith
Belfast
Odense
Bristol
Scotland
Drogheda
Bangor
Europe

Data Sheet

To the Learner

Write as many words as you can from the list you have studied, in any order. If you are not sure, you can guess.

1	_____	14	_____
2	_____	15	_____
3	_____	16	_____
4	_____	17	_____
5	_____	18	_____
6	_____	29	_____
7	_____	20	_____
8	_____	21	_____
9	_____	22	_____
10	_____		
11	_____		
12	_____		
13	_____		

Activity 4.3 Identifying features

This activity is intended to introduce learners to identifying features which can be used to classify items.

1 Ask the learners how they would decide whether certain items should be placed in the same category; that is, what features do the items in each category share? Point out that they should look for common features whenever they are categorising items. Start with a fun exercise which arouses interest: you could start by asking how the learners categorise people. They could be asked to write down the categories they use to classify other people. They may list 'caring' and 'vivacious'. Ask them to name a feature of 'caring', 'vivacious' and so on.

2 Ask the learners how CDs and tapes are categorised in shops. Ask them to identify one or more features of each category. Write the categories and sub-categories on a flip-chart. Discuss the advantages of categorisation. (Other examples which could be used, depending on the learners' interests, are categorisation of food in supermarkets or the categorisation used in discount warehouses.)

3 Give out a list of items in the learners' occupational area which have to be learned. In the catering trade, this might be wine; in the construction trade, it may be the names of materials or tools. The learners should work in pairs. Firstly, they should identify features which are common to several items; the features 'dry' and 'white' may be shared by several different wines. Then they should divide the list into categories and sub-categories on the basis of these features. If different ways of categorising are possible, there should be a short feedback session in which the relative merits of the different ways of categorising the list should be discussed.

Activity 4.4 Learning concepts

Beginners in double-entry bookkeeping programmes often have difficulty in distinguishing between the concepts 'trade purchases' and 'purchases of assets' and between 'trade sales' and 'sales of assets'. It is important that this conceptual distinction is grasped, as items classified as purchases or sales of assets will affect the total assets figure of the business, whereas trade purchases and sales will affect the profits. The following exercise in Figure 4.3, used near the beginning of a double-entry bookkeeping course, is an example of how learners can be helped to understand the new concepts by connecting them with what they already know from everyday experience. Since it starts by giving examples of each concept, you should be able to understand the exercise even if you have no experience of financial records.

The learners could be asked to complete the following figure (a hairdressing example has been filled in) before the features of the new concepts are introduced. It should be emphasised that what they are doing in this exercise – namely, thinking of examples of each new concept – can be used whenever new concepts are to be learned. They should be reminded that, if they cannot think of examples themselves, they should always ask you.

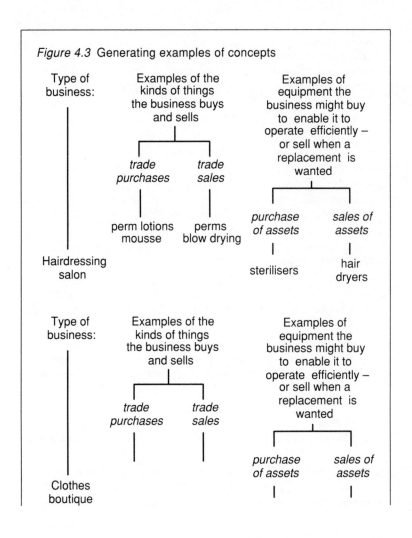

Figure 4.3 Generating examples of concepts

The features of each of the concepts ('purchases', 'sales', 'purchases of assets', 'sales of assets') could be introduced in the following way. If you want to decide whether a transaction is a purchase or a purchase of an asset, then ask yourself, why is the business buying this item? Is it:

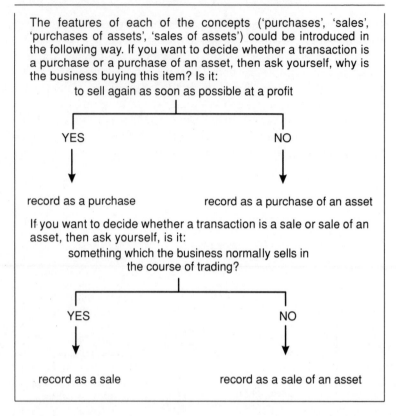

The questions above help to form a mental pathway towards a solution to the task. A sequence of questions which forms such a pathway is described as an algorithm. This brief algorithm should be used in conjunction with a list of examples (for example, a retailer of domestic electrical appliances sells (a) a washing machine, (b) a delivery van, and purchases, a floor washing machine for cleaning his premises). Before leaving this example, notice that it could be introduced with an epitomiser (see pages 46–49), or it could be related to an epitomiser which has been used earlier in the programme.

A suggested epitomiser would be along the following lines. Two of the important pieces of information a business requires are the total assets (what the business owns), which tells the business owner or manager how much is available for paying what the business owes to others, and the profit or loss. This is based on the difference between trade sales and trade purchases. For this reason it is essential to distinguish between trade purchases and sales and the purchase and sale of assets.

Activity 4.5 Organising information

This activity is intended to illustrate how information can and should be organised in memory in more than one way. By organising it in more than one way, extra routes to the information are created. More routes mean easier retrieval of information from memory.

1 Suppose that your job involves helping tourists to choose a café or restaurant and you want to be able to remember the information in Figure 4.4a (below). It will help you to remember if you reorganise it. It is organised below under the name of each restaurant. Can you think of a different way to group the information? (It could be grouped according to parts of the city and type of food.) Re-write the information using the new organisation.

Figure 4.4a Eating out in Glasgow

PJs (off Byres Road) in the West End. The food is very good, especially the spaghetti carbonara, which is among the best in the city. A la carte menu.

The Jenny Tea Rooms in Royal Exchange Square (city centre) has some of the best cakes and the best hot chocolate in the city.

The California Gourmet in Byres Road has great fast food. As well as pizzas and burgers there are massive sandwiches filled with salads. Very good value.

Pierre Victoire in Miller Street (city centre) has very high-quality food at a very good price. One of the very good dishes is salmon in filo pastry.

Café Qui in John Street (city centre) is very good for coffee and cakes.

The Hilton is excellent for French cuisine. Expensive. Comparable to the Park Lane Hilton in London.

O Sole Mio has very well-cooked Italian food. It is very quiet with very good service.

Ventura, near the Tron Theatre, does everything. Very reasonable prices and good quality.

Nico's, near the King's Theatre.

Two Fat Ladies, in the west end of the city. A la carte menu.

Mai Thai in the city centre. Sweet and sour prawn in Thai coconut sauce is excellent, as is the beef in oyster sauce.

2 Information about different types of business organisation in a text is often structured in the form of a paragraph containing information about each type, as in Figure 4.4b, which is taken from Barrow (1989).

Figure 4.4b Forms of business organisation

Sole trader

If you have the facilities, cash and customers, you can start trading under your own name immediately. There is no requirement for an external audit, or for financial information on your business to be filed at Companies House. You are personally liable for the debts of your business, and in the event of your business failing your personal possessions can be sold to meet the debts.

A sole trader does not have access to equity capital, which has the attraction of being risk-free to the business. A sole trader must rely on loans from banks or individuals and any other non-equity source of finance.

Partnership

All that is needed is for two or more people to agree to carry on a business together intending to share the profits. The law will then recognise the existence of a partnership.

All the partners are personally liable for the debts of the partnership, even if those debts were incurred by one partner's mismanagement or dishonesty without the other partner's knowledge. Even death may not release a partner from his obligations, and in some circumstances his estate can remain liable. Unless you take 'public' leave of your partnership by notifying your business contacts, and advertising retirement in the *London Gazette* you will remain liable indefinitely.

Unless otherwise stated, all the partners have equal voting rights. It is advisable to get a definition of what is a policy or voting decision, and how such decisions are to be made. You must also decide how to expel or admit a new partner.

Limited company

The main distinction between a limited company and either of the two forms of business already discussed is that it has a legal identity of its own, separate from the people who own it. This means that in the event of liquidation, creditors' claims are restricted to the assets of the company. The shareholders are

---

not liable as individuals for the business debts beyond the paid-up value of their shares. This applies even if the shareholders are working directors, unless the company has been trading fraudulently or wrongfully. Other advantages for limited companies include the freedom to raise capital by selling shares and certain tax advantages.

The text would continue by treating each of the other types of business organisation in the same way.

Learners can be shown how information can be organised in different ways by asking them after their initial reading to re-organise the information. At first it is usually necessary to provide an outline for the new organisation, such as that in Figure 4.4c.

Figure 4.4c Reorganising the text in Figure 4.4b

| *Degree of liability for debts* |
| Sole trader: |
| Partnership: |
| Public limited company:
(Other types would be entered below) |
| *Sources of capital for expansion:* |
| Sole trader |
| Partnership |
| Public limited company |
| (Other types would be entered below) |

This format would continue, with headings relating to other major categories of information, such as 'people who make policy decisions'. After completing an initial example of what is meant by reorganisation of information, learners can be asked, in relation to other topics, how the organisation of information could be altered.

Activity 4.6 Introducing learners to concept mapping

Drawing up concept structures such as those in Figures 3.1–3.6 pages 37–43 is a way of learning the mental operations which enhance organisation of knowledge in memory. Learners can be shown how to draw up concept structures for themselves. This activity is often referred to as 'concept mapping'. Further examples of concept structures appear in Figures 4.5 and 4.6. Figure 4.5 is an example of a concept structure or map which describes a stew, in that it shows the concepts that are the most probable features of a stew and their relationship to one another. You will remember that a concept map is based on categorising; that is, the main concepts are identified. In addition, the relationship of these concepts to one another is identified and labelled. Usually, it is best to begin by showing learners a completed concept map which is made up of information with which they are familiar (such as Figure 3.1 on page 37), and then to build up a new map by questioning them about another familiar area.

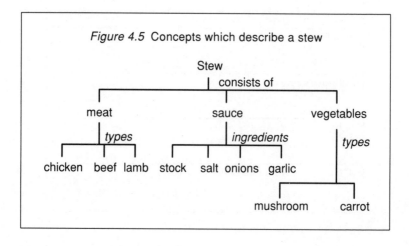

Figure 4.5 Concepts which describe a stew

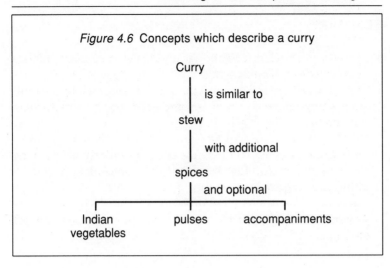

Figure 4.6 Concepts which describe a curry

Use a board or flip-chart and ask the learners to identify the main concepts, and label the relationships between the concepts as you draw the structure.

After drawing the separate structures for stew and curry, learners should be encouraged to merge the two structures shown in Figures 4.5 and 4.6 into one larger structure. Try to do this merger yourself.

Although a detailed consideration of mental operations/procedures and of the acquisition of information has been separated across Chapters 3 and 4, it is important to remember that efficient occupational problem solving depends on learners storing in memory packets of task-relevant information and procedures for major types of problems. Thus an important role for you is to devise practice problems which will encourage learners to gather together in memory packets of these different aspects of knowledge for broad categories of problems within the occupational area. If this approach permeates vocational education and training, learners will acquire many interlinked packets containing relevant information and procedures. The ultimate aim is transferability to novel situations. The key to this transfer seems to be the building of systematic practice in thinking into the vocational curriculum and using what has been learned both within and outside the occupational area.

SUMMARY

1 The way in which information is organised in memory inhibits or enhances problem solving.
2 Organisation is based on concepts and meaningful interrelationships among them. There are examples of concept structures in this chapter.
3 Every instructional activity should have a dual focus: promoting the targeted competence and the underlying thinking skills necessary for the organisation of information and its implication in problem solving.
4 This approach to teaching problem solving is based on six propositions derived from cognitive psychology. These are set out in page 35 of this chapter.

FURTHER READING

Nisbet, J. and Shucksmith, J. (1986) *Learning Strategies*, London: Routledge & Kegan Paul.
Reigeluth, C. M. (1987) *Instructional Theories in Action*, Hillsdale, NJ: Lawrence Erlbaum.

REFERENCE

Barrow, C. (1989) *The Small Business Guide*, London: BBC Books.

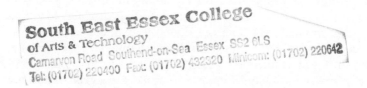

Chapter 5

Teaching mental procedures for problem solving

Efficient information learning and the interdependence of learning and problem solving was dealt with in Chapter 3. You must now focus on the other blade of the scissors, the mental operations which facilitate efficient application of relevant information to problems. As has been noted, many of the operations used in efficient learning are similar to those which increase effectiveness in problem solving. In learning a new concept like investment trust, for example, you try to identify its features and consider whether some of these are similar to a more familiar concept – such as unit trust. Similarly, you look for features of problems, and use these features to match the new problem to tasks you have successfully completed in the hope that some of the previously used operations can be used in the current problem. This means that the 'dual focus' instructional approach is equally applicable to teaching learners to apply information efficiently to solve problems. The interaction between learning and problem solving is such that, in the process of producing solutions, you often also enhance your mental repertoires, thereby increasing your effectiveness to act on the world.

You can introduce a problem-solving approach at any point in a programme, rather than waiting for a fresh intake of learners. The guidelines below will work whether you are using this approach with a group from the beginning or at some other point in the programme. Although planning instruction would usually include preparing to teach information along the lines discussed in Chapter 3, as well as its application, it is only the application which is considered for most of this chapter.

Not all instructional sessions will involve such application. There are times when you may want to focus almost exclusively on information learning, with instruction in its application following at a later meeting. If you are dealing with nursery nurses, for example, you may prefer to present information about child development at one session, illuminated by reference to examples from the learners' experience, but delay instruction in the application of this information to the next session. Obviously, what follows is more relevant to the 'application' session, the ideas in Chapter 4 being more relevant to the information learning.

In many areas information learning and application are much more entwined: in applied mathematics, working through examples is the predominant learning activity. In foreign language learning, novices master grammatical constructions mainly by using them in spoken and written phrases and sentences. In areas such as these, this chapter, which focuses on application of information, will be more relevant than Chapter 4. However, it is important not to lose sight of the principle, which is illustrated in Chapter 4, that the way information is organised in memory influences its application.

You will have no difficulty in identifying the tasks to be mastered at a particular instructional session. The form of the task will obviously vary according to the vocational area. The task may be a written one, or it may involve oral presentation of a report or activities which have to be carried out in a certain sequence. The making of chocolate éclairs is such an example; you will know of many others. Notice that mastery of a task includes being able to deal with unpredictable changes in the environment, such as clients changing their minds or electricity cuts. Mastery also involves being able to minimise the effect of one's errors. The general principles of the approach were set out in Chapter 3.

The six propositions will now be considered in relation to applying information to solve problems. For convenience, these propositions are repeated.

1 For most complex vocational tasks, including mastery of the underlying information, it is possible for experts to specify sequences of mental operations which build up into mental procedures which are necessary and sufficient to complete these tasks.
2 These operations/procedures need to be made as visible as possible to learners.
3 The teaching strategy should be such that learners are enabled

not only to store and apply the mental operations/procedures but also to generate new sequences of mental operations when required. This is the cognitive basis of thinking, which is variously described as flexible, adaptable, lateral, creative, etc. – or, as in this book, problem solving.

4 Learning of mental operations is at its most effective and most transferable when learners are consciously noting that the operations are being learned and they are encouraged to use them in a variety of learning and problem-solving tasks.

5 Regular and systematic practice in using the thinking procedures is necessary. To encourage transfer, learners should practise thinking on tasks both within their vocational area and in another area.

6 Practice should be followed by feedback dialogues in which the thinking procedure used by the learners is explored.

SPECIFY MENTAL OPERATIONS

The first proposition concerns your specification of the sequence of mental operations which are efficient for the targeted task. You would usually need some practice in becoming aware of the operations you use in carrying out tasks effectively. You should not be discouraged if, initially, it takes a long time to write a mental blueprint for a targeted task. This is simply an indication that, like most people, you do not usually make all the mental steps explicit enough to learners. The level of detail in the blueprint will depend on the mental procedures with which the learners are currently familiar. Simple examples will clarify this point.

Example one

You are trying to teach learners how to divide £100 between A and B in such a way that A has £20 more than B. If you know that the learners are competent at addition, subtraction and division of money, you do not need to re-specify these procedures. You can start the specification with the procedure for unequal division of money.

Question: Which word(s) tell you whether division is to be equal or unequal?

Answer: More than.
Question: If division is unequal, how much more is to be given to A?
Answer: £20.
Question: What is left for division between A and B?
Answer: £80.
Question: How is the £80 shared?
Answer: £40 each.
Question: How much will A receive if he has £20 extra?
Answer: £60.
Question: How can you check your answer?
Answer: By asking if £60 is £20 more than £40 and does £60 plus £40 equal £100.

The size of the steps depends on the experience the learners have had with the type of task. While the size of the steps in the specification above may be about right for the average adult learner, smaller steps may be needed for people with learning difficulties or little experience of the type of task. Level of detail and size of steps are important judgements that you must make.

Example two

Figure 5.1b describes a mental blueprint for a task which has to be mastered by accounting technicians. The task has been simplified, so that even if you do not have specialised knowledge of accounting, you can follow the specification of self-questions which facilitate a solution. The only accounting concept in the task is trade creditors, the meaning of which was explained on page 54 when concept learning was being illustrated.

Figure 5.1a Task – finding missing purchases data

Read the following and carry out the task as instructed.
   Some small traders do not keep accounts properly. Suppose that R. Wilson & Co. did not keep proper records of their trade purchases. They now want to know the total amount of trade purchases for January – December 1994. It is possible to work out the amount of the trade purchases from other information available.
   The information available which would enable you to work out the total purchases figure is:

Total owed to trade creditors at the beginning of the year – i.e. at 1 January 1994	£10,000
Total owed to trade creditors at the end of the year – i.e. 31 December 1994	£5,000
Cheques paid to trade creditors during the year January – December 1994	£18,000

The size and number of steps in the self-questions listed in Figure 5.1b would suit technicians. Obviously, they would be adjusted when the needs of particular groups are known.

Figure 5.1b Questions for finding missing puchases data

QUESTION: How does the business incur amounts owing to trade creditors?
ANSWER: Purchases of goods/materials.
QUESTION: Which amount was owed to trade creditors at the beginning of 1994?
ANSWER: £10,000.
QUESTION: In which year would these purchases have been made?
ANSWER: 1993.
QUESTION: For which year are we to calculate trade purchases?
ANSWER: 1994.
QUESTION: Is the January 1994 figure to be included in 1993 trade purchases?
ANSWER: No.
QUESTION: How much was paid out to trade creditors during 1994?
ANSWER: £18,000.
QUESTION: How much of this £18,000 is for 1994 trade purchases?
ANSWER: £18,000 – £10,000 = £8,000
QUESTION: Which figure in the problem has not been dealt with?
ANSWER: £5,000.
QUESTION: For which year's trade purchases is this amount owing?
ANSWER: 1994.
QUESTION: How does it affect total trade purchases for 1994?
ANSWER: Increases by £5,000. Therefore total trade purchases for 1993 (£8,000 + £5,000) = £13,000.

Example three

The third example concerns an organisation task. Nurse learners are expected to be able to contribute to ward organisation, bringing to bear on this task the information they have mastered during their nurse training and education. Nurse tutors frequently mention that nurse learners nearing the end of their training are not as efficient as they need to be in contributing to the organisation of a ward, and identify this as a competency which is difficult to teach. A particular problem is prioritising tasks to be done: nurse learners making up a bed for an admission expected later in the day before checking on a critically ill patient on the ward indicates poor prioritising.

The blueprint produced by an experienced nurse tutor took the form of self-questions which, if correctly answered and acted on, will lead to marked improvement in dealing with this type of organisation problem.

Figure 5.2 Questions for organising ward tasks

Which of the available staff are familiar with the ward?
Who needs immediate care?
What are their vital signs?
When were they last taken?
When are they due to be taken again?
What was the trend overnight?
Are any procedures due immediately?

It is not being implied that this is the only mental procedure for improving ward organisation. It is simply one procedure which an experienced former charge-nurse used which produced satisfactory results. What is being stressed is that the thinking steps underlying efficient performance need to be taught systematically, not left to chance. Experience will not improve performance if there is a lack of knowledge of thinking procedures appropriate to this type of problem.

The really interesting point is that these questions, with some alterations in words to suit the different situations, would cover many occupational areas.

Activity 5.1 Transferring learning

List the questions in Figure 5.2 which would be applicable (with alteration of some words) to organising staff in:

1 a hairdressing salon;
2 a restaurant kitchen;
3 a hotel dining room;
4 a nursery for pre-fives.

EXPRESSING THINKING PROCEDURES IN WRITING

The specifications of mental operations can be written in the form of lists of mental questions, or in the form of algorithms (see pages 70–1). The term 'algorithm' is used in this book to mean a sequence of questions which form pathways towards solutions. Any layout which forms pathways will do. Setting out questions in algorithmic form is used throughout the book as a way of increasing awareness of thinking processes. The form in which the specification is written is not important as long as it serves the purpose of making the mental operations visible to you and to the learners.

The following are examples of algorithms. Figure 5.3 would be appropriate for the mechanically illiterate as it deals with only the most straightforward reasons for a car failing to start. For drivers who want to advance their (car) mechanical competence the algorithm would require further questions. In Figure 5.4 a more useful question than 'Can you modify dessert?' might be, 'What modifications are possible?' This would lead to self-questions about whether time/ingredients and so on would eliminate some of the possibilities.

Can you think of other improvements to the algorithm in Figures 5.3 and 5.4? Can these improvements be expressed in algorithmic form, or would the whole thinking procedure be better expressed as a list of questions?

There is no difference in principle between specifying mental procedures as lists of questions and as algorithms. The advantage of algorithms is that they may offer a higher probability of successful performance since they give more comprehensive and precise thinking instructions. Obviously, their effectiveness depends on the degree to which the learner can answer the questions posed in the algorithm or is capable of using the instructions in the algorithm, which can point out how gaps in the

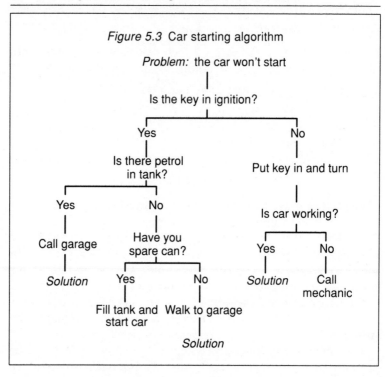

Figure 5.3 Car starting algorithm

required knowledge can be remedied. In Chapter 3 there is an extended discussion of ways of storing information in memory so that it can be retrieved easily. If information is not stored efficiently, the effect of the algorithm is limited in enhancing problem solving.

Whether or not algorithms are helpful to learners will depend on how accurately you have identified the mental operations which are most powerful in facilitating the solution to a problem. A great deal of practice is usually necessary before you can construct an algorithm which works, and learners will obviously lose faith in algorithms if their use does not improve their performance. As has been stressed throughout, the use of lists of mental questions, flow-charts and algorithms are ways of developing in learners the ability to devise for themselves thinking strategies when faced with problems. These devices are ways of indicating to the learners the active nature of thinking strategies. They are ways of modelling thinking operations which beginners or low achievers could not previously devise for themselves. Good algorithms press learners into more productive effort than they might otherwise make.

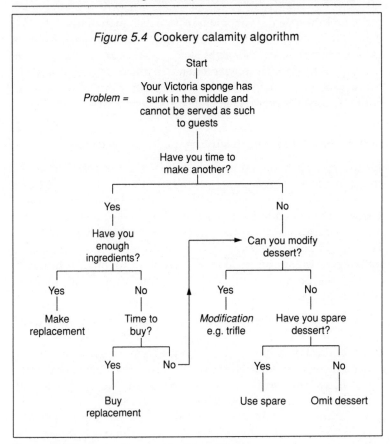

Figure 5.4 Cookery calamity algorithm

These algorithms were prepared by Alison Nimmo.

It cannot be overemphasised that lists of questions, algorithms and other forms of specifying mental procedures should never be used in a mechanical way. They are not simply a quick way of training for competence – although they are very efficient in this respect – but rather a device for introducing learners to the nature of thinking so that eventually they can generate their own mental algorithms.

At first sight this approach may strike you as being rather mechanical or overdirective. Crucial to success in using it is understanding that it is neither of these. It is sufficiently student-centred to satisfy the most progressive educator; systematic enough to win the enthusiasm of the most traditional. It rests on the assumption that people need to gain insight into how their own thinking works if they are to become efficient thinkers. It is based on research which assumes that the path to insight needs to be a structured one with many signs to guide the novice and much practice. So central is this message about the development of insight that although it was set out in the first chapter it bears repeating here.

Activity 5.2 Practice in specifying mental procedures

As the approach depends so heavily on your competence in specifying mental procedures which facilitate task performance, it is recommended that you should carry out the following activities. These are intended to help you to become more conscious of the mental operations and procedures you use to solve problems. They could also be used with learners to introduce them to the thinking processes which underlie problem solving. In this first activity, the problem is based on generally familiar information and procedures:

1 If you cannot do the problem fairly quickly, look at the end of the chapter where there is a suggested mental procedure.
2 If you think you have solved the problem, check your answer from the end of the chapter. Then try to write down the mental procedure you used. This may be in the form of a list of questions you asked yourself or in the form of a flow-chart or algorithm. Compare your procedure with the suggested procedure at the end of the chapter. Decide if your procedure is just as effective as the suggested one.
3 If possible, find a friend who cannot produce an answer fairly quickly. Teach the unsuccessful performer a mental procedure for solving the problem.

The problem, from *Herald* (Glasgow) Mind Games

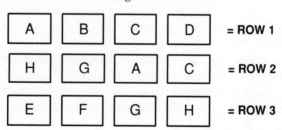

Row 1 = Four cards with different letters on both sides.

Row 2 = The same four cards from row 1, two of which have been turned over, all four of which are in different positions.

Row 3 = The same four cards from row 2, two more of which have been turned over, and all four are again in different positions for the positions they were in in rows 1 and 2.

Question: What letter is on the other side of each of the four cards in row 3?

For your second activity select one or more of the following problems and write an appropriate mental procedure in the form of questions, or an algorithm. The problems are grouped under occupational headings.

1 *Catering*: Write a mental procedure for problem (1) in Figure 1.1 of Chapter 1 (page 2). You will find a suggested procedure in Chapter 8 (pages 142–3).

2 *Caring*: A Head of Nursery reported that the nursery nurses she trains easily grasp information about ensuring the safety of children, safeguarding their health and promoting their development. Yet, when she supervises them in their work with children, she finds that they are not putting these messages into practice. They may set up an interesting developmental activity for the children but leave them unsupervised, with sharp scissors and other potentially dangerous tools in a very hot, stuffy room.

Try to write a mental procedure for planning a nursery activity which is developmental but safe. (You will find suggestions at the end of this chapter.)

3 *Engineering calculations*: Write out in the form of an algorithm or flow-chart a mental procedure for solving resistivity problems by proportion. There is a suitable algorithm at the end of this chapter in Figure 5.8.

4 Write out in the form of a flow-chart a mental procedure for solving problems involving more than one equation. There is a suitable algorithm in Chapter 9 (Figure 9.7).

5 *Beginning accounting*: A firm makes only one product, which sells for £10. The variable cost per unit is £5 and fixed costs total £75,000 per annum.

How many units does this firm need to sell just to break even? How many units does this firm need to sell to make a profit of £30,000?

There are suggested questions at the end of this chapter (page 97).

6 *Driving*: Imagine that a friend who is learning to drive has asked you to supervise her driving for an hour or so. She has had three lessons at a driving school and can stop and start the car, change gears and cope with left-hand but not right-hand turns into streets.

Write a mental procedure for selecting a route for an hour's practice in which she will attempt to repeat what she has learned at the driving school.

These procedures may be written in the form of lists of questions, flow-charts or algorithms. Try to persuade friends to write a specification so that you can compare your procedure with theirs.

7 *Text processing*: Construct an algorithm for approaching any new task in text processing and/or underlining text. You will find a suggested algorithm at the end of this chapter.

'COMPETENCES' AND MENTAL OPERATIONS/PROCEDURES

Where learners are working towards NVQs (or SVQs), competences will be prescribed by a Lead Industry Body, and you will be helping learners to achieve these competences through instruction, practice and feedback. In programmes leading to BTEC (Business and Technical Education Council) or SCOTVEC qualifications the outcomes will be prescribed in terms of behaviours which are visible and measurable. Specification of what has to be achieved in terms of competences or behavioural objectives is not incompatible with a problem-solving approach. Implementation of a problem-solving approach means that, in addition to specification of competences, there has to be a specification of the mental operations and procedures underlying the competences. As this has not been done by Lead Industry Bodies or accrediting bodies, it falls to you to specify mental operations or procedures which are to be learned and practised at each instructional session or over a period of work-based experience. Because the way that knowledge is stored in memory can inhibit or enhance problem solving, the concept structures to be learned also need to be specified in the instructional plan.

There follows a summary of how you might best proceed in

devising an instructional plan (assuming that the specification of competences or behavioural objectives already exists).

PLANNING TO TEACH THE MENTAL OPERATIONS OR PROCEDURES

Overview

Having learned to identify and describe mental operations used to acquire knowledge and deal with problems in your own occupational areas (proposition 1, page 64), you then have to write a plan for teaching these mental operations in each training session you will run. Part of this plan takes the form of a specification of the mental operations which the learners are to learn in the course of that training session.

This type of preparation for teaching is fully compatible with a competences approach. You are asked to specify as precisely as possible the concepts (that is, information), mental operations and procedures which underlie the competences, which are described in terms of observable behaviours. The acquisition of these underlying mental operations is, as far as is known, a necessary condition for transfer of what has been learned to new situations. The next three propositions (see pages 64–5) are concerned with

1 making the sequence of mental operations as visible as possible, so that the learners can see what steps they are to take;
2 doing this highlighting in ways which increase the learners' insight into what it means to think efficiently; and
3 ensuring that the learners are aware that they are forming transferable operations.

The instructional techniques required to teach mental operations are usually already known to people who have some experience of delivering vocational programmes. In this new approach the emphasis is on your using these techniques to enhance the formation of the mental operations the learners have to master, and to develop in the learners a capacity to create new sequences of mental operations when required. It is expected that you will usually be familiar with techniques such as questioning, managing discussion, giving demonstrations, setting practice tasks and giving feedback.

In this new approach it is particularly important to develop a style of interaction which

1 is non-threatening;
2 encourages the belief in learners that they can achieve more by discussing mental operations which might be used in tackling tasks, and looking for more effective sequences of operations.

EXTENDING YOUR EXISTING INSTRUCTIONAL TECHNIQUES: INTERACTING WITH LEARNERS

In this approach questioning is used to illuminate thinking procedures and to encourage their use in learning and problem solving.

Learners should be asked questions which help them to:

1 describe problems;
2 classify problems;
3 identify problems they have solved of a similar type;
4 become conscious that generalising appropriately is a useful mental operation;
5 identify features of the current problem which are similar to or dissimilar from previous problems of the same type.

You would start by presenting a problem and asking the learners what questions they could generate which would be useful in tackling the problem. The learners would be encouraged to evaluate the questions by trying them out on the problem and identifying their limitations or usefulness. A useful starting question might be, what is the most useful description of the problem? If a chef has dropped a tray of lemon sole on the floor, it is not helpful to describe the problem as 'dropped the tray of fish'. A description such as 'customers will not get the dish they ordered immediately' gives some clues as to the way forward, and may lead to questions such as: what would be the length of delay if we started to cook the sole again? Do we have any more lemon sole? Is the delay likely to be acceptable? If the answer to these two questions is 'no', can we offer a similar dish?

If it is helpful to classify the problem, questioning can be used to identify categories of problems which have previously been encountered. In Chapter 8 it is suggested that a useful classification of problems in catering is into those caused by errors and those caused by changes in circumstances outside a chef's control.

In devising your approach, the principle is one of guiding learners through the process of constructing a procedure. This is not the same as telling them. It is possible that the procedure which develops will be different from the one you have in mind, but it must be one which, in the judgement of competent practitioners, is efficient for tackling the specified type of problem. There should be no imposition of a procedure on learners, but, on the other hand, you should persist with questions and discussion of learners' suggestions until an efficient procedure is constructed. The reason for emphasising that you should prepare by constructing your own procedures is to ensure that you have a good idea of the range of mental moves which will work, for a particular type of problem.

You are required to give as much emphasis to questions about 'how to think' as you give to questions about 'how to do'. In commenting on learners' ideas or work you should emphasise questions which help learners to

1 examine the thinking operations underlying what they say or do;
2 detect the limitations of these operations and how they could be improved.

Use questioning to find out how the learner thinks about tasks and how that differs from your own more expert thinking. It is through thinking about thinking that people develop insight into how sequences of mental operations can be created when faced with problems. Above all, you have to be competent in creating a climate in which you and those who are learning from you value talking about each other's thinking: a climate where the purpose of your questioning is not just to elicit correct answers but to facilitate the exploration of thinking.

For the three tasks (Examples one, two and three on pages 65–8) you could develop understanding of thinking by guided discovery of the best self-questions. Alternatively, it could be done by modelling when you talk aloud each mental step you would take in solving the problem; for example, why is this mayonnaise too thin? Have I had this problem with other sauces? What did I do? Are there any reasons why this solution is inappropriate in this instance? You would talk about why you reject some questions and choose others, thereby indicating that some types of self-questions are more powerful than others. Another method would be to ask learners to develop the self-questions in small groups and to compare their attempts in a plenary session. These points will be illustrated later in this chapter.

MANAGING PRACTICE AND FEEDBACK

The fourth and fifth propositions on page 65 were concerned with practice and feedback. Many people are aware that a demonstration or other form of communication to learners of what is to be achieved and how it might be achieved should be followed by practice. You will be expected to be competent in selecting practice tasks for the learners and in giving feedback on their performance of those tasks. Indeed, you may have found that practice followed by feedback is the major instructional technique in many programmes, the need for taking a more direct instructional role only arising when the learner has to be introduced to some new aspect of performance. Obviously, this would be the case in work-based learning.

Although the need for practice seems very obvious in the case of practical aspects of skills like welding, report writing, cooking and so on, it is much less obvious that thinking skills which underlie performance need to be practised just as systematically. It is therefore necessary to consider how practice of intellectual skills can best be handled.

First of all, the practice tasks need to require the learner to think. This seems a very obvious point, but in many vocational programmes learners spend almost all their time practising tasks which have become so routine for them that they do not have to think about them. You need to give much more thought to building some deviant elements into practice tasks. Learners are usually capable, for example, of applying basic double-entry bookkeeping principles to the financial records of a small business by the end of an introductory financial accounts module of 30–40 hours. Practice in applying these principles is usually restricted during this module to very routine transactions. Application to less routine transactions is not usually practised until the end of a second or third module in basic accounting, but there are good reasons why the less routine should be introduced in the first module; more thinking would be necessary, and out of this thinking would come a deepened understanding of how the principles can be applied to a variety of situations.

Problems allow you to discuss mental procedures and to demonstrate how knowledge of basic principles can be manipulated to deal with a wide range of tasks. Practising on entirely routine tasks, as happens too often in the first two or three accounting modules, does not develop problem-solving skill.

In all programmes, learners can be asked to practise using some very simple but effective self-questions throughout their practice. Otherwise, many learners will refer far too many of their uncertainties to you. In further education colleges it is not unusual to see learners queuing to ask the tutor for help. They could be encouraged to ask themselves:

1 Can I think this through by recalling a similar problem, and what type of problem is it? For example, is the problem concerned with unavailability of materials? (If so – are there substitutes?) Or is the problem caused by lack of knowledge of method (or what)?
2 If so, is the tutor the only reliable informant?
3 If not, who are the other reliable informants?
4 How can I check the appropriateness of their information without referring to the tutor?

Second, learners should be conscious during all their practice that they are to be looking for appropriate opportunities to apply the mental procedures they have been acquiring. They should be encouraged, when unsure of how to proceed, to recall the mental steps they took to deal with similar tasks and to adapt these to the current problem. The concept of transfer of mental procedures – that is, generalising from one situation to another – should be discussed with learners, and they should be encouraged to perceive the ability to transfer mental procedures as a goal which is as important as other aspects of their performance. The following anecdote may help to explain to learners the importance of adapting what they learn to fit changing circumstances.

Mac, a Yorkshire terrier, looks forward immensely to his owner's return from work each day. He has learned that the theme tune from *Home and Away* predicts her arrival. He applied this information appropriately by running to the window to greet her when he heard this tune. So far, full marks to Mac for information learning and application. But can Mac apply this information in a flexible way to suit changing circumstances? One evening Mac's owner was home early, long before the beginning of *Home and Away,* but as that theme tune started Mac rushed just as enthusiastically to the window!

In order to develop the ability to transfer as widely as possible, consideration should be given to making time available for learners to tackle some problems outside their own occupational area. Learners pursuing a catering programme could be given some problems in the caring area. The discovery that much of the thinking in relation to customer care can be transferred to caring for the elderly helps to develop insight into the nature of transfer. Learners should also have opportunities for practice in transferring the more general mental operations such as categorisation to tasks outside their own area. In Chapter 7 there is an extended discussion of transfer.

As is the case with setting practice tasks for learners, you will be aware that feedback on performance on those tasks makes an important contribution to learning. Feedback is no less crucial in developing the thinking skills which underlie problem solving. When you give feedback on practical skills it is usually based on the learners' performance, which is more visible to you than their thinking. Feedback often takes the form of suggestions about changes in the learners' actions; for example, 'Increase the pressure ... stand nearer to the weld ... press that key'.

Although there are many similarities in giving feedback on performance and feedback on thinking, there are also some important differences, which mean that you have to acquire some additional feedback techniques. Whereas both you and the learners usually take it for granted that feedback has a central role in learning practical skills, there is generally no such assumption on the part of the learner with regard to thinking skills. Unless learners believe that some aspect of an instructional situation will help them to learn, they are unlikely to co-operate wholeheartedly. In the development of thinking skills, wholehearted effort and commitment from the learner are essential.

It is therefore necessary for you to set aside some time to discuss with the learners the notion that errors in performance are often symptoms of errors in their thinking. If errors in thinking are not remedied, they will impede the achievement of competence. Examples should be used to illustrate this notion, and it should be emphasised that improvements in thinking are highly amenable to instruction. Many learners make errors in maths problems because they classify the problem wrongly, which leads them to select the wrong procedure, or they miss out steps in the procedure because they do not sufficiently monitor themselves in applying it to the problem. Many shortcomings in dealing with customer's requests in restaurants and hotels arise from employees misinterpreting what the customer wants, or failing to consider all relevant factors in deciding whether the customer's request can be met and whether an extra charge is to be made. Learners should be encouraged to understand that they need to make their thinking as well as their actions visible. This means being willing to talk to you and to one another about their thinking.

It follows from what has been said in the previous paragraph that you need to ask learners questions which help them to reveal how they thought their way through a task. While it is always important to create a non-threatening, psychologically secure atmosphere in any training activity, the creation of an ethos of acceptance and respect is particularly important in teaching thinking skills. Since the general culture places a high value on intelligence, revealing one's thinking is a risky business, psychologically speaking. It is important from the outset that questions are posed in a normal conversational style which invites exploration, rather than in the tone and manner of a person who is 'an authority and in authority'.

You may be very good at formulating questions which take learners forward, but are not nearly as effective as you might be because the tone of the interaction is one of interrogation rather than exploration. You need to communicate that learners' responses are not treated as right or wrong but rather as starting points. When learners reveal thinking which is inappropriate for a problem, they can often best be helped to modify it by questions from you, rather than you saying, 'This is how I think it through'. However, modelling in this way is not ruled out, as it may be the most appropriate technique in some circumstances.

The following conversation between a restaurant manager and a learner illustrates the ongoing nature of a problem-solving approach.

At 1.30 p.m. the manager notices that one of the learners is about to fry sole *goujons*:

MANAGER: What is your serving time?
LEARNER: 2.30 p.m.

MANAGER: How long does it take to fry sole *goujons*?

LEARNER: Two or three minutes.

MANAGER: What are you going to do with the *goujons* after you have fried them?

LEARNER: Keep them hot.

MANAGER: What changes are likely to take place in the *goujons* between now and 2.30 p.m.?

LEARNER: I'm not sure.

MANAGER: What happens to food if it is kept hot for a long time?

LEARNER: dries out . . . cooks some more . . . oh! they might taste like rubber . . . OK.

Food preparation in a training kitchen provides many opportunities to use a problem-solving approach. A key to your success is to persuade the learners to keep asking themselves what they can learn from what is going on around them as well as from their own activities. Where four groups of learners are preparing different dishes, there are opportunities to ask questions of their peers. They will only do this if you have made it clear that this is a legitimate and beneficial thing to do, and if the learners know the most useful questions to ask each other – for example, how did you know that your whiting was ready to serve? Quite often people identify and remedy their own thinking errors when they are given the opportunity, and your role is then to confirm that the learner has worked out a more effective mental procedure.

At the centre of a problem-solving approach should be constant opportunities for learners to assess the effectiveness of the procedures they use in tackling problems and to suggest improvements. This means that you have to make opportunities for the learners to talk about their procedures and to identify clearly weaknesses in procedures which made them inefficient in relation to a completed task. Many of you would say that you do this. The evidence suggests that mostly you do not go far enough. In programmes which produced significant gains in thinking skills, tutors were careful to check that learners could give an explicit account of the critical features of more adequate procedures and, if necessary, help them to construct such an account.

How this approach was put into practice by a nurse tutor is described in the following outline and commentary.

A Outline: tutor's preparation

1 *Describe the problem which is to be the focus of the instruction*:
Student nurses are to identify patients who have actual or
potential pain.
2 *Draw up the mental blueprint*: Specify the thinking procedure
which will significantly increase the probability of a successful
solution. Sequence of questions to be drawn up in the form of
an algorithm (see Figure 5.5).
3 *Select the instructional techniques: guided discovery and
small group discussion followed by tutor-led discussion*:
   (a) Introduce the student nurses to the notion of mental procedures. *Note*: This introductory exercise is not required
in subsequent work, when the student nurses have grasped
the idea of mental procedures.
   (b) Help student nurses to develop mental procedures for the
vocational problem.
4 *Facilitate transfer of learning.*
5 *Arrange practice with feedback dialogues.*

Commentary on preparation and implementation

1 *Describe the problem which is to be the focus of the instruction*:
Student nurses are to identify patients who have actual or
potential pain. As explained at the beginning of this chapter,
the acquisition of the underlying information is not being
dealt with in this chapter – the focus of instruction is the
mental procedure for applying the relevant information – the
assumption at this point being that the information has been
stored efficiently in memory. Information learning was discussed in Chapters 3 and 4.
2 *Draw up the mental blueprint*: The nurse tutor's preparation began
by specifying – as clearly as possible – mental steps that made up
a thinking procedure which, when implemented, would significantly increase the probability of a successful solution. You will
find it useful to remember that no specification can guarantee
success at complex tasks for all of your learners. Self-questions
require self-answers, and a selection will have to be made from
several possible answers. A good specification of mental steps
is a highly useful guide to success rather than an assurance of
an effective solution. Figure 5.5 shows the nurse tutor's own

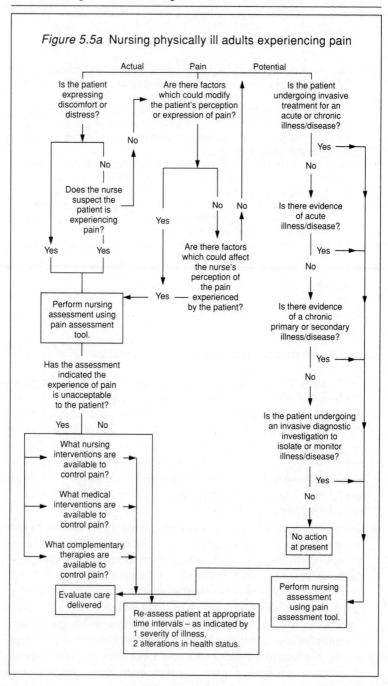

Figure 5.5a Nursing physically ill adults experiencing pain

Figure 5.5b Nursing physically ill adults experiencing pain
(algorithm)

In drawing up the blueprint you must make a number of judgements. Some of these are about how general or specific the initial algorithm is to be, what follow-up algorithms will be used, and about the level of detail necessary for the learners. The nurse tutor had to decide if the student nurses were familiar with mental procedures for detecting evidence of chronic illness/disease and whether there was a need to incorporate questions for detecting chronic illness/disease into the algorithm. All the steps in a specification should be taught initially, albeit in stages, if it is, as in this case, a lengthy one. After the learners have practised applying all the steps to solve problems, the algorithm (or list) can sometimes be condensed by combining several questions into one, which does the work of several in the overall procedure.

---

specification of an appropriate sequence of questions. In subsequent meetings more specific algorithms would be developed for pain assessment, nursing interventions, medical interventions and complementary therapies. There would then be branching off from these more specific algorithms.

3 *Select the instructional techniques: guided discovery and small group discussion followed by tutor-led discussion*:

(a) *Introduce the learners to the notion of mental procedures*: The nurse tutor began by explaining to the student nurses that people need to learn how to think if their practical problem solving is to improve. She asked them to start to learn by considering some problems in everyday life, which require generally familiar information plus a sequence of mental operations for bringing the information to bear on the problem. For each problem, she asked them to work in pairs to produce a list of the questions they might ask themselves to solve the problem. One of the problems they worked on was as follows:

You are baby-sitting one evening and the parents have forgotten to leave a contact phone number. The baby's nappy needs changing but you cannot find any nappies in the house.

Individual student nurses volunteered questions, the others being asked to comment on the usefulness of the questions and whether they needed to be altered until a set of questions had been agreed and written on a flip-chart. Possible answers to the questions were considered so that the student nurses would understand that, in a practical problem-solving situation, they would need to be able to generate further questions in response to each of their answers. Eventually the list of questions in Figure 5.6 was agreed.

Figure 5.6 Dealing with shortages of materials

- Do I know someone who has a baby – and transport?
- If no: are there any local suppliers open?
- If yes: could I phone a friend who would obtain a supply? If no:
- What are the desirable properties of a substitute for a nappy? (Very low cost – therefore disposable – leak-proof, comfortable, can be safely attached to baby)
- Do any items in the house have all these properties? e.g., kitchen roll. If no:
- Which properties are missing? (e.g., in the case of kitchen roll, comfort; in the case of bath towels, low cost requirement)
- Is there any way of compensating for the missing properties?

(b) *Help learners to develop mental procedures for the vocational problem*:
(Note: the problem of identifying patients who have actual or potential pain was introduced, and the student nurses said that this was difficult for them even though they had acquired relevant information about causes and alleviation of pain at various points in their nurse education.)

Firstly, the nurse tutor asked the student nurses to work in small groups of 4–5 in order to generate their own sequence of self-questions for the problem. At this first session, the nurse tutor expected, at the feedback discussion from the small groups, to guide them towards the questions on Figure 5.5 which start from the 'actual' (pain) section of the algorithm. At the next session, the nurse tutor, through discussion, tried to establish the questions which follow from the 'potential' (pain) section. At subsequent sessions, this guided discovery approach was repeated so as to take the student nurses on to the construction of more specific algorithms for pain assessment and interventions. By the end of each discussion the agreed questions had been written on a flip-chart and the student nurses took away copies of the questions. You may find this a helpful way for your learners to record the outcome of their discussion.

You will find that it is common for novices in small group discussions to generate more questions than there are in your (the expert's) blueprint. This is because novices have not yet learned to identify the questions which have the potential for retrieving more information relevant to the problem. The obvious drawback of using more self-questions than necessary is that long lists are difficult to remember. When learners produce a large number of self-questions, they can be encouraged, during the led discussion, to find one question which helps them to retrieve as much relevant information as four or five of the questions in their list.

When the learners have identified, through small group and led discussion, the most productive self-questions – and sequenced these questions – you should then discuss with them whether it would be most useful to record the questions for future reference in the form of a list or in some other form. It is usually beneficial to introduce the algorithm presentation of mental procedures through a task with which learners are thoroughly familiar. This can be done through a guided discovery method. You might, for example, show and talk the learners through an algorithm for multiplying or dividing by two figures, and then guide the learners in constructing an algorithm from the 'pain' problem questions which have been developed. Guided discovery should be used in conjunction with a flip-board or chalk-board to demonstrate how the questions can be arranged in the form of an algorithm. Learners should make, or be issued with, a copy of the agreed algorithm (or list). There are two main reasons for this:

1 learners tend to attach significance to written notes or handouts;
2 learners forget a great deal from one day to the next – the written record helps them to put into practice what they have learned.

4 *Facilitate transfer of learning*: Learners should be encouraged to think of problems of a similar nature which they have encountered and to suggest if any parts of the solution

procedure can be generalised to these other problems. In the 'pain' problems, categorisation was used: actual and potential pain; patient and nurse perception of pain. This operation could be transferred to other problems where it is helpful to break the problem into components.

5 *Arrange practice with feedback dialogues*: Learners should be set to work, first on simulated problems in the classroom (e.g., case studies), and then on real problems in the workplace. You should emphasise to them that they are to go through all the thinking steps in the algorithm. Some learners are reluctant to put themselves to what they consider additional effort. One way you can help to ensure that the algorithm is used is to issue to each learner several copies of the algorithm, and to ask them to use a fresh copy of the algorithm for each problem, ticking off each step in the algorithm as it is performed. This also helps to raise the status of the algorithm by signalling that evidence of its use is expected and valued as much as the end result. Obviously, this is more practicable when the learners are working on case studies, and other simulations such as role play, than in the work situation.

The next step for the nurse tutor would be to reach agreement with the student nurses that on their next spell of ward experience they would keep with them a summary of the agreed questions and to try to use these questions when this problem arises. The nurse tutor should also try to secure the student nurses' agreement that they will use this approach to develop mental procedures for other problems which they encounter in the ward.

Persuading others

Time should be set aside as soon as possible after the practical experience for your learners to discuss with you the extent to which the use of the prepared mental procedure facilitated practice and to consider their suggestions for modifying or extending the procedure. Time should be allowed also for discussing their experiences of applying the approach to other work-based problems. Obviously, making such arrangements for discussion is often far from straightforward. A commitment to negotiating such arrangements is necessary if the development of problem-solving skills is to be more than fashionable rhetoric. The approach is most effective when everyone who has a role in learners' training uses the feedback dialogues discussed in this chapter. (See also the discussion of practice and feedback on pages 78–82.)

It is essential that this kind of approach should be used throughout a vocational education programme. It needs to be used consistently in order to provide enough practice in thinking so that learners use a thinking approach as easily as they would use other well-practised skills.

ALTERNATIVE STEPS FOR IMPLEMENTING THE APPROACH

Modelling mental operations

In the student nurse example, the students were introduced to the notion of building up procedures for thinking by working in small groups to produce self-questions, first for a simple, everyday problem and then for the work-related problem. Another way of introducing the approach is for you (the expert) to demonstrate how you think your way through problems. Obviously, you would need to prepare by unpacking your thinking before the instructional session to make sure that you had identified appropriate thinking procedures. Although few of you would dream of teaching practical movements without some kind of demonstration of the task, you may be unaware that it is often necessary to demonstrate mental operations. If learners are to have an effective springboard for later innovation in their thinking, you need to become aware that you should be trying to demonstrate the nature of rational thinking in your occupational area. Thus, you must extend your demonstration techniques in ways which allow you to show the learners how you think – namely, modelling the mental operations. This will involve you in learning to talk aloud your own thought processes, so that these can be heard and understood by the learners. By thinking aloud about the questions you would ask yourself in planning, in carrying out and evaluating the outcomes, you are demonstrating what is involved in thinking.

Example

Figure 5.7 shows the modelling of appropriate mental operations for the first stage in preparing a paper which has to be based on a lengthy government-sponsored report or on textbooks. Note that the questions are not set out in algorithm form.

This example was provided by a local government officer working with administrative officers who had problems in assimilating fairly lengthy reports which affect the performance of their work roles in areas such as housing, economic development and environmental health.

Activity 5.3 Modelling self-questions for understanding reports

Before you look at Figure 5.7 you should try to talk aloud the sequence of questions you ask yourself in trying to assimilate lengthy documents in your own occupational area. If possible, ask a friend to write what you say. If your mental procedure is significantly different from Figure 5.7 is it because the documents or papers you are required to read are different from the policy/social issues type for which the Figure 5.7 mental procedure was obtained – or is there some other reason?

If possible, try to compare your mental procedure with that of others in your own occupational area. Are there still significant differences between your colleagues' mental procedures and your own? If so, try to list reasons for the differences.

Figure 5.7 Acquiring information from lengthy reports

There would be constant use of the question 'Is this making sense?'
If not:

- 'How can the meaning be clarified?'
- from surrounding text?
- from another text?
- from another person?
- by recalling from memory similar ideas/procedures/situations, etc. and comparing with current text?

On a first reading – scan

What is the writer trying to do?

- argue a case?
- give information?
- describe procedures?

If presenting an argument:

- Is it in agreement with my views?
- if not: What are the differences?

If providing information:

- What's new to me?
- Do I need to check sources?

On second reading – identify main points/features

- Where is the comment on each point/feature?
- What is the relationship between points/features and supporting evidence?

Is it:

- causation?
- sub-category?

How adequate is the evidence?
What are the criticisms?

On third reading

Can I summarise in own words?
What are the implications for own work or concerns?

- for others' work and concerns?

Which committees are involved?
What is the cycle of meetings?
Is there to be a response?

- to whom?
- what time scale?

What resources are required to complete the task?

Guided discovery of mental operations

This technique for helping to communicate appropriate mental operations and procedures was mentioned in the student nurse example. A variant of this technique would be that, instead of the learners working in pairs to generate self-questions, the session could take the form of your introducing a problem and working with the whole group. You would ask for suggestions of appropriate questions the learners might ask themselves to get started, to progress towards the solution, to monitor their progress and check the accuracy or appropriateness of their solution. Learners would be encouraged to comment on one another's suggested questions. The discussion would be guided by you towards efficient mental operations by asking questions, if the learners themselves do not pose them, which point to inadequacies in suggested sequences of mental operations.

More direct instructional techniques

There are few hard-and-fast rules about education and training. For some tasks and some learners it may be appropriate to present your own algorithm to them rather than involve them in its construction, provided that it is done a step at a time and the learners have an opportunity to discuss each step before proceeding to the next. Direct instruction is usually more appropriate when introducing complex technical procedures for the first time. On subsequent problems of a similar type the guided discovery method described on page 91 can be used, which involves the learner more in the construction of the algorithm. A variant of guided discovery is, of course, starting the task of algorithm construction in small groups, as described on page 86.

A POSTSCRIPT ABOUT INTELLIGENCE

In Chapter 2 there was a very brief reference to the nature of intelligence. Over the last ninety years there have been many attempts to say what intelligence is and how it develops. From this research many different theories have arisen. Now that we have explored what is meant by concept structures and how these structures connect with each other to make up meaning and mental procedures, you will be better able to assess whether the following description of intelligence fits in with your own everyday experience of learning in solving problems.

> The components of intelligence are knowledge, organised into interconnected concept structures and into mental procedures which facilitate application of the concept structures and problem solving.

This description is consistent with current research into thinking in problem solving. There are still huge uncertainties about many technical questions concerning how our vast repertoires of knowledge and procedures are stored in memory and how they change as a result of our reading, listening, thinking and acting on the world.

What must be stressed is that, if the above description of intelligence is accurate, then intelligence is learnable and teachable. Individual differences in rate of learning which is observed in people can be explained to a significant extent by factors such as:

1 the person's relevant prior knowledge of what has to be learned;
2 the range of mental procedures the person has acquired;
3 the way the new subject matter is organised by you or presented in written learning materials;
4 the extent to which you explicitly teach the mental procedures for using knowledge.

If, as research suggests, people's learning and problem solving can be improved, managers, educators and trainers should be working for this improvement rather than acting on an assumption that people's intelligence is fixed by their biological makeup, an assumption which has never been adequately supported by evidence.

SUMMARY

1 *Identify non-routine tasks* which have to be mastered if the learner is to be judged as competent.
2 *Specify a series of mental operations* (a mental procedure) which, if correctly implemented, will produce acceptable task performance. The specification may be in the form of a list, or some kind of flow-chart or algorithm.
3 *Decide how the mental operations are to be learned*:
   (a) by the tutors modelling mental operations for tackling problems (including learning);
   (b) by a guided discovery through tutor-led discussion;
   (c) by discovery through small group discussion followed by tutor-led discussion in the larger group (e.g., the learners would work first in small groups on the task of specifying the most efficient mental operations for a given problem; they would consider suggestions from one another and select a final list for discussion with the whole group);
   (d) by tutors presenting/discussing mental operations (where

tutors are dealing with fairly technical problems it may be helpful to present a sequence of mental operations one at a time, and to apply each operation to the problem under consideration).

4 *Provide learners with a written record of agreed mental procedures.*

5 *Provide practice on tasks which deviate in some ways from routine elements*:
   (a) tasks within the learner's occupational area;
   (b) tasks outside the learner's occupational area.

6 *Provide feedback: plan feedback dialogues*: There should be considerable emphasis on helping the learners to diagnose and remedy 'bugs' in their own thinking. Although learners need feedback on the discrepancy between the quality of their own output and that of a competent practitioner, they need to know also how their thinking should be adjusted if they are to improve as quickly as possible. If learners make errors, this usually reflects a failure of the learners to ask themselves appropriate questions – therefore plan to ask learners to explain their own thinking to you.

7 *Prepare back-up material*: Prepare handouts showing main points if the lesson has included new information.

SUGGESTED THINKING PROCEDURES FOR THE TASKS IN ACTIVITY 5.2

1 *Herald* (Glasgow) Mind Game

What information provides a start?
There are four cards which have the letters A B C D on one side (row 1).
On the reverse are the letters E F G H (row 3).
Rows 1 and 2: which cards remain the same?
∴   A and C remain same side but moved (row 2).
∴   (H and G) are on the other side of B and D.
Are there other position differences from rows 1 and 3?
All four are in different positions.
∴   Since B is above G
    B = H
    G = D

Then
Rows 2 and 3: consider only E F
(E and F) = (A and C)
All changed position.
A cannot = E (same position)
$\therefore$ A = F
and C = E.
(This solution was prepared by Sheena Holmes, Lecturer, Scottish School of Further Education, Strathclyde University.)

2 **Planning a nursery activity which is developmental but safe**:
Which children will participate?
Developmental needs?
What can they do at present but only with adult help? (e.g., sort shapes? count things? follow instructions? pretend?)
Which of these goals most/least interests the children?
Are there other criteria for selecting a goal? (What kind of achievements would facilitate further development? Are the children going to school soon?)

Planning the activity
How much time is available for the activity? For the preparation?
Do we already have an appropriate activity which could be modified?
Which activities would best promote the identified needs?

• which of these can be planned with the resources available?

Which of the activities identified as promoting the developmental goal is

• most interesting for the children?
• will give most benefit for time invested by staff and children?

Safety
Which tools/materials are potentially dangerous?
What kinds of misuse of tools/materials by the children might bring about accidents?
What kind of supervision is needed? (e.g., how many children can each adult supervise at each stage of the activity?)
Which children are least likely to follow safety rules?
Does the room temperature need adjusting?
Should windows be opened?

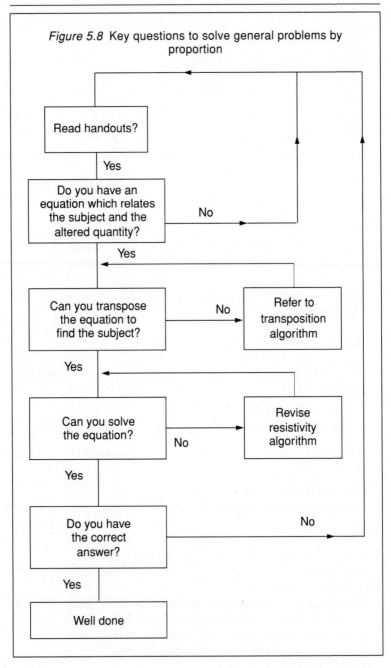

Figure 5.8 Key questions to solve general problems by proportion

4   *Figure 5.9* Questions to solve a basic costing problem

What is meant by break-even? (no profit, no loss)

How much does it cost to make each unit? (£5 the variable cost)

What is left over from the selling price of each unit after the cost of making it is met? (£10 – £5 = £5)

How much are the fixed costs? (£75,000)

How much can come from each unit sold towards the fixed cost total? (£5 per unit)

Thus the number of units to be sold to cover the total fixed costs is: total fixed costs ÷ £5.

$$= \frac{£75,000}{£5} \quad = \quad 15,000 \text{ units}$$

15,000 units is break-even point.

What happens to the £5 per unit left after variable costs have been met and fixed costs have been met from the sale of the 15,000 units? (profit)

How many extra £5s are required to make £30,000? (£30,000 ÷ £5) = 6,000 units, therefore to make £30,000 profit 6,000 + 15,000 = 21,000 units need to be made.

(There are other shorter sequences of questions which would suit learners who are more mathematically sophisticated.)

FURTHER READING

Francis, H. (1991) *Individuality in Learning*, London: Further Education Unit.

Greene, J. (1987) *Memory, Thinking and Language*, London: Methuen.

Landa, L. N. (1974) *Algorithmization in Learning and Instruction*, Englewood Cliffs, NJ: Educational Technology Publications.

—— (1976) *Instructional Regulation and Control*, Englewood Cliffs, NJ: Educational Technology Publications.

—— (1984) 'How do we teach novices to perform at expert level?' *Contemporary Educational Psychology* 9 (3): 235–45.

Lerner, I. Y. A. (1980) *The Process of Instruction and its Laws*, Moscow, Znanie.

McGuiness, C. and Nisbet, J. (1991) 'Teaching thinking in Europe', *British Journal of Educational Psychology* 61: 174–85.

Smith, L. (1986) 'Ability learning: an analysis of Piaget's theory of ability in adolescence', Further Education Unit Occasional Paper, London: Longman.

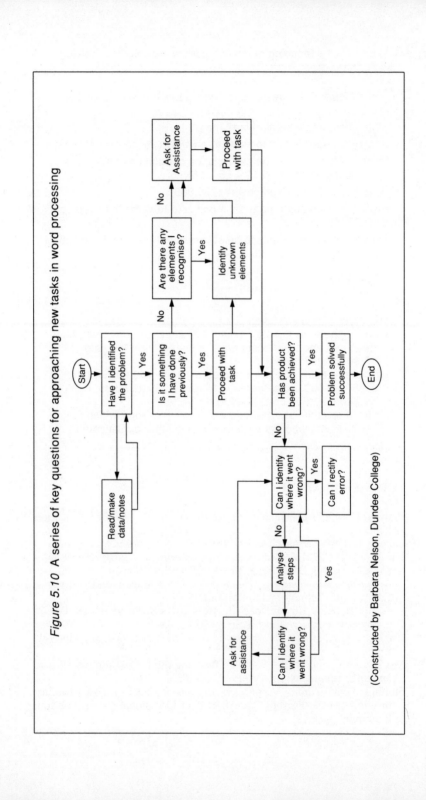

Figure 5.10 A series of key questions for approaching new tasks in word processing

(Constructed by Barbara Nelson, Dundee College)

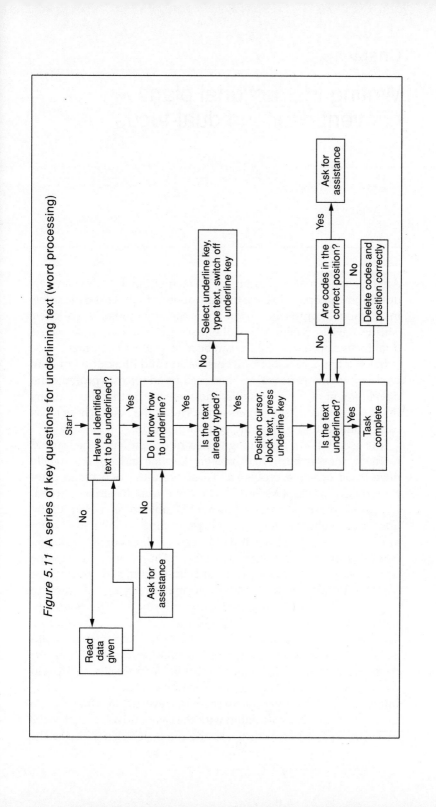

Figure 5.11 A series of key questions for underlining text (word processing)

Chapter 6

Writing instructional plans – conventional and dual-focus

Anyone who has had training in facilitating learning and in developing people will have thought about and practised planning instructional approaches, even if it is the often unfairly maligned 'sitting next to Nellie'. If 'Nellie' uses the previously described dual focus approach, 'Nellie' can be a very effective trainer.

In Chapters 2 to 5 there was discussion and illustration of how well-known instructional methods can be adapted to promote the development of thinking skills, and there are further illustrations in the more specialist chapters at the end of the book. These ideas can be built into the planning you normally do.

It is useful in your planning to describe what has to be learned by the learners in terms of *information learning* and *learning to apply information* to solve problems. These were the two broad categories used in Chapters 3 to 5 to describe what has to be learned. If you use these categories, you will be able to refer back to the appropriate chapter for ideas on promoting a problem-solving approach. Using these two broad categories does not preclude you from combining information learning and application in the same instructional activity. Sometimes it is interesting and effective for learners to learn certain kinds of information through attempts to apply it. This can be done by issuing information sheets accompanied by mini case studies and questions about the case studies. The points made in Chapter 4 about encouraging mental organisation through categorisation of information would still apply: concept maps could be drawn up by the learners after they had completed the mini case studies. The ideas in Chapter 5 could be implemented by asking the learners to construct an algorithm to guide their thinking in dealing with the case study. Concept maps and algorithmic type charts are the main vehicles to make the learners conscious of the possibility of working out mental procedures for learning and problem solving. You should also plan discussion to identify other situations in which the mental operations can be used.

A SUGGESTED TUTOR PREPARATION SHEET

Please note that all the steps listed below will not be applicable to every instructional session.

Analysing and specifying what has to be learned – the mental blueprint

1 Information learning
2 Learning to apply information

Both (1) and (2) involve learning or adapting mental procedures.

List the concepts which are new for the learners. If the explanations of these concepts involve using other concepts which may not be familiar enough to learners, these other concepts should also be listed beside each to-be-learned concept. For example, if learners are to understand the concept of debtors, they need to understand that sales on credit involve delayed payment. If they are to learn the concept of current assets, they need to understand the concepts of debtors and stock, and other concepts which are covered by the term 'current asset'.

Draw a simple concept map showing relationships (where applicable)

1 between new concepts;
2 between new concepts and other concepts which are relevant and known to the learners.

(Concept maps are discussed in Chapter 4.)

Plan to emphasise any features of the new concepts or tasks which would help learners to remember them; for example, concept: 'readiness' of white fish: feature(s): fish flakes when pressed.

List examples or analogies (if any) which would help the learners to understand the new concepts.

Write mental procedures which will facilitate

1 learning the information initially – e.g., from your lesson/ demonstration (see Chapter 4);
2 revising the information from a handout in a way which will help learners to retrieve it later for applying to problems (see Chapters 4 and 5);
3 applying the information to tasks you have set (see examples of lists of questions and algorithms in Chapter 5).

> ### Selecting instructional techniques and sequencing activities
>
> (See Chapters 4 and 5.)
> Write the sequence in which the information and supporting activities or techniques will be used. The analysing and specifying which you have already carried out will show the main to-be-learned concepts and procedures.
>
> ### Plan the learners' practice and feedback
>
> Make provision for facilitating transfer. Anticipate thinking errors so that you can be ready with questions (see Chapter 5).
>
> **Plan written support materials** (notes, algorithms and so on)

Rather than offering complete 'instruction plans', the differences between planning for conventional and planning for 'problem-solving' teaching will be illustrated through consideration of sections of such plans. Steps are suggested for those who want to use this problem-solving approach.

The following examples compare the 'dual focus' approach with a conventional approach.

EXAMPLE ONE

Many restaurants try to increase their turnover through promotional schemes which involve customers paying a lump sum – say, £20 – to join the scheme in return for price reductions on meals, provided that certain conditions are met. It is desirable to run an instructional session for waiting staff who also calculate bills so that costly errors are avoided. This session would aim at ensuring that the staff will acquire, retain and apply the information about the often complex conditions for price reductions. An example of a promotion appears in Figure 6.1.

In a traditional instructional session you might pick out and explain the important points on an overhead projector, asking questions to check understanding and to emphasise particularly important points. The important points are shown in Figure 6.1. Learners would then be given details of food consumed by different customers and asked to calculate bills. The term 'student-centred' is often used to refer to a variation of this method which omits or cuts down on tutor presentation of information. For this

Figure 6.1   Rules for discounts at the Grapevine,
27 Main Street, Bothwell, Glasgow G71

A   12 LUNCH OFFERS

You and your guest are invited to enjoy one Complimentary Fixed
Price Lunch, when a second Fixed Price Lunch of equal or greater
value is purchased, up to twelve times before expiry date.

(Maximum value £6.95 per card per visit.) Valid Sunday to Friday.

B   9 DINNER MAIN COURSES

You and your guest are invited to enjoy one Complimentary Dinner
Main Course, when a second Dinner Main Course of equal or greater
value is purchased, up to nine times before expiry date.

(Maximum value £9.50 per card per visit.) Valid Sunday to Friday.

C   12 BOTTLES OF HOUSE WINE

You and your guest are invited to enjoy one Complimentary Bottle of
House Wine when you spend over £15 on two Main Courses, up to
twelve times before expiry date.

(Maximum value £8.25 per card per visit.) Valid Sunday to Friday.

D   3 DINNER MAIN COURSES

You and your guest are invited to enjoy one Complimentary Dinner
Main Course, when a second Dinner Main Course of equal or greater
value is purchased, up to three times before expiry date.

(Maximum value £9.50 per card per visit.) Valid Sunday to Friday.

BONUS OFFER

You and your guest are invited to enjoy two Complimentary Desserts
on your first visit. This offer is combined with offer B, C or D.

(Maximum value £4.90)

Upon presentation of your **V.I.P. Card**

YOU MAY CHOOSE ONLY ONE ITEM FROM
A, B, C OR D PER CARD PER VISIT

Rules of use
- Not to be combined with any other offer or promotion.
- Maximum of 2 cards per party.
- Bank holidays, New Year's Eve, Valentine's Day, Mother's Day,
  Father's Day and December 11th to 24th inclusive excluded.
- Non-refundable. Lost cards cannot be replaced.
- Offer valid for six months from date of purchase.

Figure 6.2 Algorithm for calculating discounts on lunches

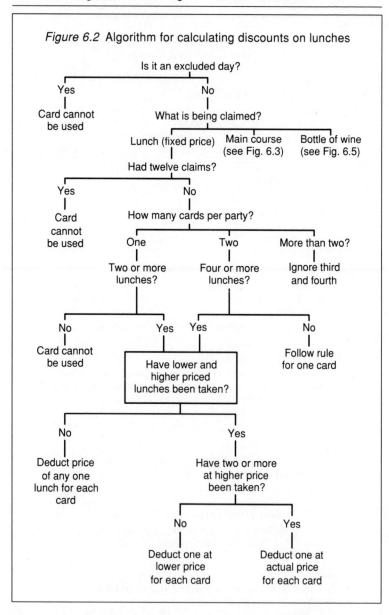

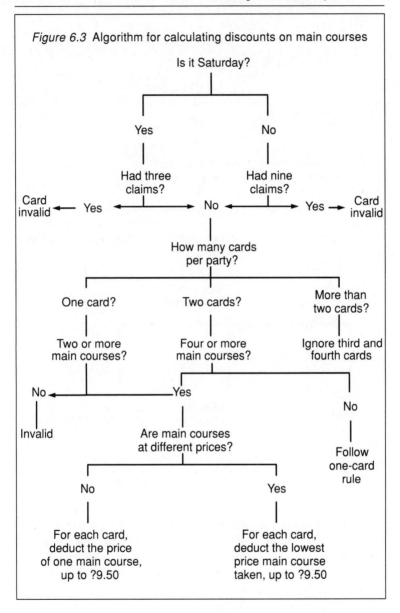

Figure 6.3 Algorithm for calculating discounts on main courses

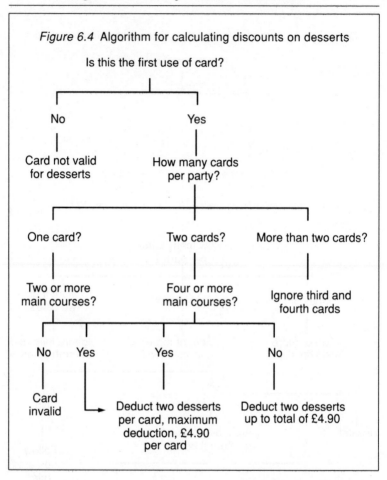

Figure 6.4 Algorithm for calculating discounts on desserts

particular session, the 'student-centred' instruction would probably involve issuing sheets covering the information about the promotional scheme (as in Figure 6.1) together with food orders for which bills are to be calculated. However, this does not go as far as the approach outlined in this book.

In an instructional session in which the aim is to develop thinking skills as well as proficiency in applying the information about price reductions, you might begin by asking the learners for their ideas about how they could most efficiently master the information. Learners would be encouraged to identify

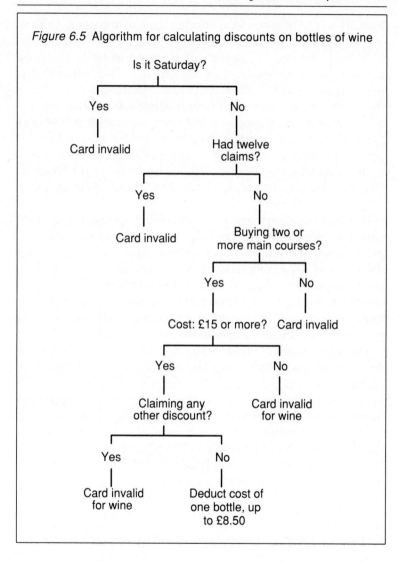

Figure 6.5 Algorithm for calculating discounts on bottles of wine

advantages/disadvantages of suggestions, and you would help the learners to implement the soundest ones. Alternatively, or additionally, you might give out the information in Figure 6.1 on a printed sheet, and suggest that the learners work in groups to produce an algorithm which, correctly applied, would lead to the correct solution for most circumstances. An algorithm could also be worked up through discussion led by you (see Chapter 5). The learners would be given food bills to calculate in order to test and revise the algorithm and to practise applying the new information.

Towards the end of Chapter 3, the point was made that good problem solvers have wider task-relevant information than poorer performers. For this particular task another difference would be the inclusion of wider information about the advantages/disadvantages to the business of the price reductions in the sales promotion scheme. Simple information about fixed and variable costs in producing and serving meals would help the learners to understand why the scheme could be beneficial to the business. This broader understanding may secure greater effort in implementing the scheme.

In both a traditional and problem-solving approach you might issue the information and the bill calculation tasks and omit your presentation of input. However, in the traditional approach, your focus would be on completion of the task, whereas, in a problem-solving approach, there would be the additional focus on the construction of a mental procedure. The aim of this focus is to make explicit to the learners the thinking operations and the possibility of using these operations in other tasks.

The achievement of problem-solving skills is increasingly being required in vocational modules, but the suggested 'student-centred' instructional approach is not very different from conventional instruction. Notably, there are often no suggestions about how to coach the problem-solving skills.

The tutor preparation sheet suggested at the beginning of this chapter would be completed as shown below for Example one (training waiting staff to apply appropriate reductions to bills when the promotional card is presented).

Analysing and specifying what has to be learned

What has to be learned can be described as follows: information about the conditions relating to price reductions; advantages and disadvantages to the business; mental operations for applying the information in calculating restaurant bills; identifying situations where similar operations can be used. The new concepts are fixed and variable costs.

The concepts which make up the information about conditions for reductions are familiar to the learners, since these are categories from the normal menu.

Mental procedure(s): prepare algorithms for applying the information (see Figures 6.2–6.5), so that the range of thinking steps which are efficient for the task are known.

Selecting the instructional techniques

Discuss advantages/disadvantages of discounting to the restaurant. Omit your presentation of conditions, and issue these on a printed sheet since there is only a small quantity of information and it is made up of familiar concepts. The learners are to learn it through construction of an algorithm in small groups, followed by a plenary discussion led by the tutor. Learners will then modify their own algorithms in the light of this discussion.

Plan the learners' practice

Issue restaurant bills to be calculated; learners will check that their completed algorithm works for these bills.

Plan feedback dialogues

Anticipate learners' difficulties in constructing the algorithm and plan questions to guide their thinking. Plan discussion to identify other situations in which the mental operations may be used.

Other examples which could follow this pattern could be instruction about certain aspects of employment law and contract law. The quantity and complexity of the information would be greater, as also would be the question about its application. A traditional instructional session on these matters would proceed along the lines described on page 102 – you giving a modified lecture with learner support material followed by practice. Alternatively, but still within a conventional approach, the learners might be set a reading assignment which covers the to-be-learned information, after which they might answer questions or participate in discussion and/or deal with mini case studies.

EXAMPLE TWO

This shows some parts of an instructional session which uses the advocated 'dual focus' approach in relation to the aspect of (Scottish) law of contract, which deals with the effect of innocent misrepresentation on a contract. The learners are assumed to be HNC students working towards NVQ level 3 accreditation. The main differences in this example between a conventional approach and the 'dual focus' approach is:

your concept maps (Figures 6.6, 6.7 and 6.8);
construction of concept maps by learners;
an algorithm which will guide the learners' thinking when they are trying to

1 learn from tutor exposition,
2 learn from a book,
3 revise the information;

discussion of other topics to which this dual focus approach could be applied.

Analysing and specifying what has to be learned

1 *Information learning*:
   innocent misrepresentation: definition; effect on contracts
   new concepts to be learned during 1 hour period:

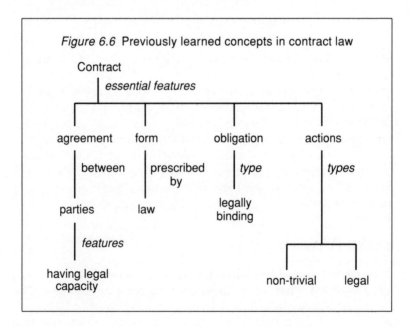

Figure 6.6 Previously learned concepts in contract law

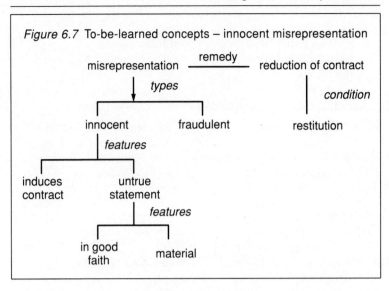

Figure 6.7 To-be-learned concepts – innocent misrepresentation

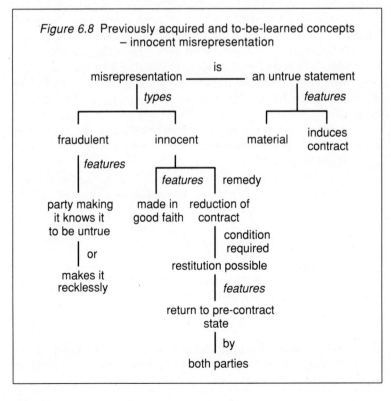

Figure 6.8 Previously acquired and to-be-learned concepts
– innocent misrepresentation

voidable
misrepresentation, innocent and fraudulent
reduction of contract
restitution.
2 *Learning to apply information*:
learning to apply information to mini case studies.

Figure 6.6 shows a concept map for already learned concepts
which are directly relevant to this instructional session. Figure 6.7
shows the to-be-learned concepts, while Figure 6.8 shows a map
which combines the already known and to-be-learned concepts.

Emphasis of features of concepts:

Concepts are learned most efficiently by storing their main *features*
in your memory (see Chapter 4). Your instruction will be most
efficient when you highlight the main features which give the
concept its meaning. For example, one of the most important
concepts used in the legal definition of innocent misrepresentation
is 'material' – the untrue statement must relate to a 'material'
aspect of the contract. The main feature of 'material': is to be a
substantial aspect of what is being done under the contract, not a
relatively unimportant detail. You can highlight features by
presenting exemplars – instances of the feature – and non-
exemplars, which are definitely *not* instances of the feature. For
example:

Exemplar: Z has entered a contract to sell X a new car of a certain
make or model. Any misrepresentations about engine capacity are
likely to be 'material'.

Non-exemplar: Misrepresentations about the colour of the up-
holstery might not be 'material'; exemplars and non-exemplars
for each feature/concept would be listed in the preparation.

Mental procedures to facilitate:

1 learning the information initially – see Figure 6.9;
2 revising the information from a handout; ask learners to construct their own concept map of all aspects they have covered of
   contract law;
3 applying the information – see Figure 6.10.

Case studies would be provided. Learners would be guided by
tutor-led discussion to construct a set of questions or an algorithm
which would work for the case studies.

Figure 6.9 Learning questions: contract law

This suggests what the learners should be doing (mentally) when they are trying to learn the information initially.
Is this a new category/sub-category of information? If so, can I label it? Can I think of:
• another exemplar and non-exemplar for each of the new concepts/features?
• situations which clearly meet all the conditions required to establish innocent misrepresentation?
• situations which are less clear-cut examples of the conditions required to establish innocent misrepresentation?

(There are further questions which would be identified by law tutors.)

Figure 6.10 Applying questions: innocent misrepresentation

The beginning of a mental procedure to apply the information to case studies in which one of the parties may or may not be able to establish the conditions for reduction of the contract.
• Which of the necessary conditions for innocent misrepresentation seem to be
present?   absent?
• What additional information would help to establish the conditions which seem to be
present?   absent?

Use a mental procedure such as Figure 6.9 to revise features of a legal contract, thereby providing practice in how to learn this type of information. Ask learners to continue using the procedure (mentally) while the concepts are being discussed; for example, innocent misrepresentation, its remedy, the features which distinguish it from fraudulent misrepresentation. Fairly clear-cut examples from everyday experience as a consumer would be used to illustrate each essential feature of innocent misrepresentation.

Learners should offer for discussion both clear-cut non-exemplars which lack one of the essential features, and also situations which are fuzzy and need further information before a decision can be made. Learners should suggest further information which would help to clarify whether each situation is an exemplar or non-exemplar.

Learners should then construct concept maps which connect innocent misrepresentation with previously learned information about contracts. Through tutor-led discussion or in small groups they should also construct a mental procedure which will work for the case studies (see Figure 6.10).

Practice would take the form of written responses to mini case studies.

Feedback dialogues could focus on written responses to case studies. For example, there could be questions about thinking errors such as the following: Did you miss out a step in the mental procedure? Did you produce an inadequate response to one of the procedural questions?

EXAMPLE THREE

An area which benefits from the 'dual focus' approach is text processing, particularly with regard to displaying text effectively; for example, four-column statements, sales literature, programmes of social events for clients. If you work in this area, good conventional practice would usually include extensive questioning by you to emphasise efficient steps towards achieving an acceptable layout, but the role of self-interrogation to achieve effective display is little used.

In applying the 'dual focus' approach in this area two major ideas from Chapters 4 and 5 would be used. One is the use of an epitomiser (Chapter 4) in introducing display work. Figure 6.11 shows the kind of concepts which would be introduced in the epitomiser through a variety of examples of both well displayed and poorly displayed work which would be provided by the tutor.

Figure 6.11 An epitomiser for displaying text

In relation to each piece of displayed work, what effects are achieved by:

space left blank, at sides, top and bottom, between columns or items?

items typed close together or far apart?

type face selected – bold, italic?

The second major idea, from Chapter 5, is the emphasis on self-interrogation. Figure 6.12 shows the beginning of a short list of

Figure 6.12 Questions about layout

What is the overall purpose of the document?
What is the most important information in the document, the next most important, etc?
Which pieces of information in the document need to be read together to make sense?

Figure 6.13a Layout of an advertisement

RECRUITING?

Use the Society's *Appointments Memorandum* to advertise
job opportunities to your fellow members.

By advertising here, you *know* you are reaching
only qualified psychologists and students on approved courses
– currently some 16,000 persons –
a guarantee no other publication can make.

CLASSIFICATIONS

- Educational
- Psychotherapy
- Teaching/Research
- Forensic (*new*)
- Not classified

- Clinical
- Occupational
- Counselling (*new*)
- Psychology Graduates
- Franchises: and other business proposals (*new*)

- Overseas

For full details, rates, copy deadline schedule,
telephone 0533 549568 and ask for the
Appointments Memorandum.

questions which could be developed through tutor-led discussion and which could be used for most display work.

The following comparison of a 'dual focus' and a conventional instructional session where the objective in both cases is to develop competence in effective display of statements with three or more columns shows similarities and differences between these approaches.

You may find it useful to think through the questions in Figures 6.11 and 6.12 in relation to the advertisement in Figure 6.13a.

In both approaches you might begin by showing some examples of three- and four-column work which is reasonably well displayed. You might go on to ask questions to emphasise important features of the display, which are in each case that the left and right hand margins are similar and also, in each example, that the spaces between the longest word in each column are equal.

Learners would be issued with a four-column statement similar to Figure 6.13b which they are to display effectively.

Figure 6.13b A four-column statement

	Alpines		
	Colour	*Flowering time*	*Situation*
Rosea	Pink	Late spring	Any sunny soil
Bell flower	Blue	Summer	Any soil
Thyme	Lavender	Summer	Sunny
Golden rod	Yellow	Autumn	Well-drained

Conventional approach

You might use questions to emphasise each stage of a method for achieving an acceptable display. You might ask the learners to:

1 find the total letter spaces which will be occupied by the word(s) in each of the longest columns – e.g., 43;
2 subtract this total space required from the number of spaces on the paper to be used – e.g., A4 'landscape' 100 – 43 = 57;
3 allocate the space left over between margins and inter-column spaces: two margins plus three inter-column spaces – i.e., 5 blocks of 'white space'.

You might then explain that if all five blocks of space are to be equal, the left-over space already calculated will be divided by 5 – e.g. 57 ÷ 5 = 11 (+ 2). This will give the starting point for the first column (11 spaces in from edge of A4).

If the margins are to be wider than the inter-column spaces you would explain a method for deciding on width of margins and point out that, by subtracting the margins (for example, 2 x 15) from total left-over space (57), they will arrive at the space available for distributing between the columns. Thus, if 30 spaces for the two margins is subtracted from a total left-over space of 57, then 27 spaces are left. If three inter-column spaces are required, 27 is divided by 3, allowing 9 spaces between each column. It would be pointed out that the starting points for each column could be found by the following method:

Left hand margin	=	15
Add		
Width of first column	=	10
Add		
Inter-column space	=	9
Second column starts at		34 (15 + 10 + 9)
Add		
Width of second column	=	8
Add		
Inter-column space	=	9
Third column starts at		51 (34 + 8 + 9)
Add		
Width of third column	=	11
Add		
Inter-column space	=	*11*
Fourth column starts at		73 (51 + 11 + 11)
Fourth column ends at		85 (73 + (column width) 12)
End of fourth column:		85 + 15 (margin) = 100

The dual-focus approach

The learners might be invited to generate questions which would help in constructing a method for tackling this problem. They might suggest or be led, if necessary, towards formulating a question about the sub-goals they need to achieve in displaying

Figure 6.13a. A sub-goal would be establishing the starting point for each column. They could be encouraged to ask what relevant information is available or could be readily established (for example, space available, space required and space left over). Another type of question the learners would be encouraged to raise would be one about criteria or constraints (in this case criteria or constraints relating to distribution of space between columns and margins). The learners should be deciding in the light of criteria whether margins and inter-column spaces are to be equal.

SUMMARY

Important features of the approach:

1 Embedding problem-solving skills in vocational programmes.
2 Identifying and teaching the mental operations underlying the vocational competences.
3 Facilitating learning in ways which help learners to develop insight into the nature of their own mental processes, in order that the learners will become able to construct a sequence of mental processes for themselves when faced with problems – tasks which are different in significant respects from ones they have already mastered.
4 Developing consciousness that this is how problem solving works.

FURTHER READING

Francis, H. (1991) *Individuality in Learning*, London: Further Education Unit.
Glaser, R. (1984) 'Education and thinking: the role of knowledge', *American Psychologist* 39: 93–104.
Greene, J. (1987) *Memory, Thinking and Language*, London: Methuen.
Howard, R.W. (1987) *Concepts and Schemata*, London: Cassell.
Landa, L. N. (1974) *Algorithmization in Learning and Instruction*, Englewood Cliffs, NJ: Educational Technology Publications.
—— (1976) *Instructional Regulation and Control*, Englewood Cliffs, NJ: Educational Technology Publications.
—— (1984) 'How do we teach novices to perform at expert level?' *Contemporary Educational Psychology* 9 (3): 235–45.
Lerner, I.Y.A. (1980) *The Process of Instruction and its Laws*, Moscow: Znanie.
McGuiness, C. and Nisbet, J. (1991) 'Teaching thinking in Europe', *British Journal of Educational Psychology* 61: 174–85.

Nisbet, J. and Shucksmith, J. (1986) *Learning Strategies*, London: Routledge & Kegan Paul.

Reigeluth, C.M. (1987) *Instructional Theories in Action*, Hillsdale, NJ: Lawrence Erlbaum.

Smith, L. (1986) 'Ability learning: an analysis of Piaget's theory of ability in adolescence', London: Further Education Unit Occasional Paper, Longman.

Chapter 7

Transfer and assessment
Rocky roads to travel

UNDERSTANDING TRANSFER

Transfer occurs when prior learning contributes to solving subsequent problems, the term 'problem' being used, as it is in this book, to include learning. 'Transfer involves learning something in one situation and applying it in another' (Blagg and Lewis 1993). As discussed throughout this book, the components of the 'something' which is learned are concepts and procedures. When people are confronted with a problem, they need to select from memory concepts and mental operations those which can serve as the intellectual building blocks of a solution. It is commonly assumed that transfer somehow just happens. One of the clearest messages from research is that this is not the case. Research demonstrates that we have to learn to transfer our learning from one situation to another. This means that transfer is unlikely to happen unless promoted systematically through instruction until it is mastered by learners. The errors at work described in Chapter 2 could easily have been avoided if the performers had asked themselves a few questions which should be well practised in vocational education.

Different degrees of transfer have been described in terms of 'near' and 'far' transfer. An example of near transfer would be the situation where the original learning involved adding two-digit numbers and the next learning task involved adding three-digit numbers. In far transfer there are more substantial differences between the original task and the new one, and/or the similarities are less visible. An example would be where the original task had involved number problems (such as $4 + ? = 9$; $(5 \times 4) - ? = 18$) and the new task involved arithmetic word problems (for example, Ben had 9 sweets and he gave some to Dan; Ben now has 4 sweets left. How many has he given to Dan?). The differences between the number and the word problems are more substantial than the differences between the two problems which use numbers only. It is less obvious that some of the mental operations used in number problems can also be used in the word problems.

The word 'obvious' is the important one in the last sentence. Almost all tasks will share some elements, in the sense that they will be amenable to solution through using some of the concepts and mental operations used in other tasks. If you were set the task of learning the Russian alphabet, you might start by looking for a feature in each letter to help you to remember it. Or you might first look at all the letters and then classify them on the basis of ones made up of straight lines and ones which have only curved shapes. The point being made is that, while it may not be obvious that this task shares elements with tasks you have learned previously, efficient performance can be achieved by using feature detection and classification, mental operations you use very frequently. In other words, you can transfer these operations from one problem to another. You can use feature detection in a wide range of tasks. It is particularly useful in monitoring your own performance. There is anecdotal evidence that many new diesel car-owners occasionally fill their cars with petrol, which is an expensive error. You can avoid this by looking for features which confirm you are filling with diesel. The obvious feature is, of course, that the pump is usually labelled, printed in black. You can quickly detect that you are using the correct fuel if you listen for a distinguishing feature of diesel running into a tank – it sounds softer, more treacly than petrol. A difficulty which many people have with transfer is that very often they do not notice that what a new task and a familiar task have in common is that similar mental operations can be used.

It is useful to think of near and far transfer as a continuum, with near transfer at one end, representing situations where the procedure required in two tasks is very similar; for example, transfer of learning to add two-digit numbers to learning to add three-digit numbers. At the other end of the continuum is far transfer, where the mental procedures used in one task must be substantially supplemented or modified in order to produce a solution for a second task. For example, in arithmetic word problems, mental operations are required which are additional to those required for similar problems stated entirely in numbers.

Still further is the transfer involved in using a body of knowledge which has been acquired in a higher education setting in solving problems at work.

In the previous chapters there has been considerable emphasis on tackling problems by developing sets of self-questions. You can see from one of the examples discussed in Chapter 5 on page 68 and reproduced in Figure 7.1 how these self-questions contribute to transfer of what has been learned in solving a problem in one situation to solving a similar type of problem in quite a wide variety of other situations. The set of questions in Figure 7.1 was developed with student nurses to help them to organise tasks in a hospital ward. They can be used with minor alterations in solving many other problems.

Figure 7.1 Organising ward tasks

- Which of the available staff are familiar with the ward?
- Who needs immediate care?
- What are their vital signs?
- When were they last taken?
- When are they due to be taken again?
- What was the trend overnight?
- Are any procedures immediate?

The same type of question, with alterations to the specific words, could be used for managing a hairdressing salon or a food production kitchen. Similarly, mental procedures for diagnosing a car fault could be adapted for use in a variety of occupations, in that some of the questions in the procedure will have the aim of eliminating certain hypotheses. Clearly, this type of elimination question has uses beyond fault diagnoses in cars. An obvious application of the type of question which is designed to eliminate possibilities would be in medical diagnoses.

Another type of mental procedure applied in medical diagnoses uses the notion of probability. Vets who are trying to diagnose the cause of symptoms in a six-year-old cat might ask themselves questions about the most probable diseases in this age group, and whether the cat's symptoms match any of these diseases. This type of probability question might be used in a variety of other situations.

If problem solvers have stored a large number of mental procedures, and if each procedure can be used with appropriate modifications in a variety of situations, they will have in total quite a large repertoire of thinking skills. The remaining problem for the problem solver is to bring these procedures, when appropriate, to bear on tasks. As noted at the beginning of this chapter, there is little evidence that this happens unless steps are taken consistently to make learners conscious of their mental procedures and their applicability in many situations. Since it is important that possible procedures spring to mind easily, constant practice in developing and adapting procedures is essential.

PROCEDURES FOR MANAGING OTHER PROCEDURES

In addition to the many mental procedures you learn, there is a need to learn a special variety of procedures which can perform the function of orchestrating the selection and use of procedures. Different terms are used by different theorists to describe procedures which perform this orchestrating function. All of the terms have connotations of co-ordinating and managing. Like a manager or captain of a team, these special procedures make the best of our cognitive repertoire, using strengths to compensate for weaknesses. Thus these special procedures have been described as 'superordinate', 'executive' and 'managerial'. 'Meta-cognition' has been one of the most widely used words to describe a person's consciousness of the potential availability of all aspects of their knowledge and procedures and how they can be effectively deployed.

There is an interesting body of evidence which supports this idea that 'managerial' procedures have an important role in problem solving. Derry and Kellis (1986) found differences in the 'superordinate' procedures of low-achieving soldiers and high-achieving college students: they demonstrated that the deficits could be remedied through a training programme which targeted the 'superordinate' procedures. The Derry and Kellis programme was introduced in the context of arithmetic word problems. After the soldiers were taught these 'superordinate' procedures, which help to bring in the most appropriate other procedures and to monitor and adjust task performance, their achievement scores increased dramatically.

EMPLOYMENT DEPARTMENT PROJECTS

Five projects were funded by the Department in the early 1990s, which gave particular attention to investigating the kinds of learning activities likely to foster the ability to transfer what has been learned in one situation to another.

The main findings are summarised in an Employment Department publication, 'Thinking and learning at work', produced by Nigel Blagg and Rachael Lewis (autumn 1993). In participating in one of the projects, 'Thinking skills at work' (TSAW),

> trainees were encouraged (during the final part of each TSAW session) to talk about the learning points and thinking skills highlighted during the session and consider where else they might be useful in the workplace . . . trainees were helped to abstract any principles and rules . . . applicable to a wide range of situations.
>
> (Blagg *et al.* 1993)

One of the early problems in the TSAW Administration, Business and Commerce Module involves processing business calls, scheduling appointments and effective customer management (Figure 7.2). At the end of each instructional period there is 'transfer' discussion. The trainees are asked to consider what they have learned about listening, asking questions and ways of being sensitive to customers. They are asked to say what general rules they have learned, such as that planning their own work involves understanding other people's priorities. Notice that this emphasis on understanding more general principles ties in with the point made in Chapter 3, that research suggests that good problem solvers have a better grasp of broad principles. Blagg *et al.* (1993) found that 'there was good evidence of trainees transferring the principles into their workshop, employment context and/or wider learning environment'.

Research carried out as part of the 'Learning in Context' project (summarised in 'Thinking and learning at work') addressed the issue of whether it is better to teach problem-solving skills 'solely within the trainees' current occupation or teach skills within varied occupational contexts' (Wolf *et al.* 1990).

Work was carried out with 56 YT schemes and around 1,000 trainees from retail, hairdressing, clerical, catering and painting

Figure 7.2 Task from TSAW Administration, Business and Commerce Module

MON 8 APR 11.05

I've been ringing and ringing and ringing ! Your switchboard is constantly engaged. How many lines do you have? It's absolutely imperative that I meet with Mr Powell today.

Good morning it's John Smith from Peaks Bank here—Mr Powell wanted to discuss an investment loan as soon as possible. When could our representative call to see him?

I've got to see Mr Powell—I'm phoning from Rotherham—there's a chance of a big order if we move fast. I'll be back tomorrow afternoon. Book me in, will you?

Good morning, TraffiCom. Yvette speaking, how may I help you?

REEVES *Assurance*
MEMO
To Whom It May Concern

You may find it helpful to know how Mr Powell likes to structure his day:
Meetings: 1 hour
Interviews: 30 minutes
Working day: 9.00-5.00
(Friday): 9.00-4.30
Lunch: 1.00-2.00
Daily admin: 9.15-10.00
NB: Days leave Thurs 11th

Good luck with the new job.

Clare

This is Communication Services. I'd like to see Mr Powell early this week. Morning if possible.

Cooper here, from Atchen. I'd like an appointment with Mr Powell to discuss new contracts with your company. I'd prefer Wednesday morning.

This is Bill from Electro Components. I'm returning your call about a possible meeting between Mr Powell and our Managing Director. Would Wednesday or Thursday morning be convenient?

Hello, its Mrs Powell speaking. Can I pop in to see my husband this afternoon? It's rather important.

Appointments this week:	Wed 10th
Mon 8th	
10.15-11.15 Mr Gould	10.15-10.45 (Mr Swale)
2.30-3.30 Mr Truman	**Thurs 11th**
Tues 9th	**Fri 12th**
2.00-2.30 Micro-Tec	3.30-4.30 staff meeting

How would you deal with each telephone call?
Record your replies. Complete the appointments schedule for Mr Powell for the week beginning Monday 8th April.

© 1993 Nigel Blagg Associates

Transfer is also encouraged through a 'Master Juggler Checklist' used by trainees in every TSAW activity. The checklist contains self-questions such as:
What does the problem remind you of?
What have you done before that might help here?
Are things going according to plan?
How will it help you if you involve others?

Source: Blagg *et al.* (1993)

and decorating/general building [trades] .... The project designed training and assessment exercises which simulated ...
commonly recurring problem solving activities (stock control,
allocation of time slots, budgeting) required in many jobs. ... A
final group of trainees received no special training and served
as controls.

(Wolf *et al.* 1993)

One of the experimental groups received problem-solving training which focused on relevant problems within a range of occupations (including their own). Another group was given activities
focusing on similar problems but solely within their own occupational context. Both groups performed better on problem-solving
tests within their own occupational area than the trainees who had
received no problem-solving training (namely, the control groups).

What is of particular interest is not just that trainees' problem-
solving performance can be improved through participating in
problem-solving activities, but that the experimental group which
had practised problem solving on tasks from a range of occupations performed better when faced with fresh problems in an
occupational area they had not encountered in their training than
the groups which problem-solving training had been restricted to
their own occupational area. The trainees who received the varied
training across a range of occupational contexts also did as well
as, or significantly better, in their own occupational context, than
the group which had been exposed to problem-solving training
only in their own occupational area. These results suggest that
improvements in transfer, brought about by varied training, are
not achieved at the expense of poorer problem-solving performance in their own area. It is well worth looking at 'Learning
in context: patterns of skills transfer and training implications',
Wolf *et al.* (1990).

While each of the TSAW modules (Blagg and Lewis 1993)
primarily relates to one broad occupational area (catering, administration or engineering), 'individual activities are designed to
involve a number of different job roles'. In addition, tasks from
each of the TSAW modules have applications in various employment contexts. This helps trainees to become aware of the use of
the thinking skills they are learning not only in their own job role,
but also in other jobs across an industry or organisation. Activities
in the TSAW Catering Module cover budgets and menu plans,

stock control, managing customer enquiries, bookings and schedules, complaints and problems, dealing with emerging situations
and identifying and remedying failures in health and safety
regulations. Many of the activities provide useful simulations for
GNVQ courses in leisure and tourism as well as health and social
care. The Engineering Module covers similar broad themes and
skills but in an engineering context. Also included are activities
designed to improve skills in visualising and analysing shapes
and structures, skills required in interpreting diagrams, all of
which are much needed in engineering. In addition to problem
solving, all of the TSAW modules include activities to promote
GNVQ core skills development in the areas of communication,
application of number, working with others and improving their
own learning performance. The activities in the TSAW modules
make extensive use of illustrations, a feature which makes the
ideas more accessible to trainees who regard reading as a tedious
chore. A drawing showing a chaotic boatyard scene (Figure 7.3)
is used in the Engineering Module for an activity which is
designed to develop and apply thinking skills to organisational
systems, efficient working practices, health and safety and customer care. Trainees are asked:

'What issues need attention in the boatyard? How would
you deal with them if you were the Workshop Manager,
Company Accountant, Union Representative, Health and Safety
Officer?

The booklet 'Thinking and learning at work' summarises
Malcolm Craig's projects on 'Training in Fault Finding and
Diagnosis'. Six open learning modules were developed and, in
common with the other Employment Department projects, 'the
modules ... address recurring issues relevant to a range of
(varied) industrial contexts. The materials are broad based and
aim to help employees to generate the questioning, problem
solving strategies and principles which underpin successful fault
diagnosis in any industry'. Like all of the Employment Department projects reported here, Craig's study encouraged transfer
by using a holistic approach 'which emphasised the interaction
between all processes and all personnel ... involved'. This
holistic approach to fault diagnostic training was developed
'instead of concentrating on specific fault finding behaviour'.

Figure 7.3 Task from TSAW Engineering Module

 What issues need attention in the boatyard? How would you deal with them if you were the Workshop Manager, Company Accountant, Union Representative, Health & Safety Officer?

© 1993 Nigel Blagg Associates

Source: Blagg *et al.* 1993

These project reports emphasise the need for tutors to receive additional training, designed to foster understanding of the points which have been made about transfer in this chapter, and of how thinking skills can be developed through vocational education and training. Trainers in the TSAW project (Blagg *et al.* 1993)

completed self-appraisal questionnaires about their attitudes towards trainees and about their approach to training. This part of the study showed that TSAW trainers became more optimistic about the capabilities of their trainees, more positive about their role as trainers, more aware of and committed to important factors in training for transfer. Since the beneficial effects of high expectations are well documented [these findings are important].

It was noted in Chapter 2 that evidence is accumulating that intelligence, in the sense of efficient thinking, is amenable to improvement through education and training. The TSAW findings suggest that the additional training which the TSAW trainers received helped them to understand this view of intelligence better.

ASSESSING THINKING AND PROBLEM-SOLVING SKILLS

It is quite difficult and time consuming to design valid instruments for assessing problem-solving skills, valid in the sense that they succeed in measuring what they claim to measure: problem solving within a vocational area. This is due in large part to the complexity of these skills. As has been emphasised throughout the book, problem solving involves a complex interaction between your information about something and your thinking procedures. Validity is not an all-or-nothing matter, but more a matter of validity for a particular purpose. What is being considered in this book is teaching vocational problem-solving skills. Therefore the purpose of the tests considered in this chapter is mainly to find out whether learners' problem solving in vocational areas improves after exposure to problem-solving training. If you would like further information on assessing thinking skills, you will find the following reports of great value: 'Measuring "Broad" Skills' (Wolf 1993); and 'Measuring Broad Skills: Guidance on Assessment Procedures' (Wolf, in press). Strongly recommended also is the 'Learning in Context' report (Wolf *et al.* 1990), because it contains full details of the tests used to measure transfer of thinking skills from one occupational area to another. The areas covered are the retail, hairdressing, catering, clerical and painting and decorating trades. One of the tests used for hairdressers, including the instructions for the person who was carrying out the test, is reproduced in Figure 7.4.

Figure 7.4 Allocation one: hairdressing tester's guide

1 This exercise involves drawing up a plan showing arrangements in a hairdressing salon.
   Go over the information sheet [see page 132] with the trainee.
   Explain the way appointments have been made for today: e.g., 'Clare is booked to do a cut and blow-dry with Mrs A at 9.00, a perm with Mrs B at 9.30' and so on.
   Explain appointment intervals, giving an example of each (explanation scripted: see information sheet for procedures). 'I would like you to rule out a page for booking in the appointments for today. Mark in appointments already made with Clare, Fiona, Tom and Sharon. You should draw the plan so that further appointments can be added.'

   If trainees ask for help, do not give advice, or answer yes or no to specific questions. Say: 'You should use the information on the sheet to decide what to do.'
   If a trainee asks about CBDs or perms, you may repeat the examples, but do not paraphrase or give other help.
   Give the trainee plenty of time to insert the appointments, then ask: 'Can you just read through the information sheet once more and see if there is anything you want to change or add to your sheet before we continue?'
   Changes made?

   START THE CLOCK

2 'A customer, Mrs T, phones up wanting a cut and blow-dry as early as possible. Use your plan to see what time you could offer, and with whom.'
   Trainee's time . . . . . .   Stylist . . . . . .
3 Mrs U phones up wanting a cut and blow-dry with Clare. She cannot come in until 11.00, but would like it as soon after 11.00 as possible.
   'What would you offer her?'
   Trainee's time . . . . . .
   Give the trainee plan three (a completed booking sheet), saying: 'This is the way the manageress draws up a booking sheet. I'd like to see how you get on with adding to her plan.'

---

4 'Mrs V phones up, wanting to know the time of the earliest available appointment for a cut and blow-dry with Tom. What time would you offer?'

Trainee's time . . . . . .

If necessary (Yes/No) tell the trainee 'Mrs V decides to come at 10.30.'

'Mark in Mrs V's appointment.'

If wrongly marked in (Yes/No) tell trainee to correct plan.

5 'Mrs W would like to be fitted in for a cut and blow-dry before 11.30. She is fussy about who does her hair and wants to know which stylists are free, and at what time.'

Trainee's offer(s): Fiona at 10.00/Clare at 10.30 other (specify): . . . .

If only one time is offered, prompt (Yes/No): 'Is any other appointment possible?'

Trainee's time . . . . . .   Stylist . . . . . .

'Mrs W chooses the 10.30 appointment with Clare. Mark this in.'

If wrongly marked in (Yes/No), tell trainee to correct plan.

(Further questions follow to test ability to identify options exhaustively/find best option/recognise repercussions of change.)

9 Mrs Z comes in wanting a perm today. Can you fit her in, and if so with whom and at what time?

Trainee's answer: 'No'
                     'Yes': time . . . . . .   Stylist . . .   . . .

If trainee suggests Fiona, prompt (Yes/No): 'Mrs Z isn't keen on Fiona. Can she have a perm with Clare or Tom?'

Trainee's answer: 'No'
                     'Yes': time . . . . . .   Stylist . . . . . .

If yes, tell trainee there is in fact not enough time (but don't explain).

10 'While Mrs Z thinks about coming in tomorrow to see Clare or Tom, Miss L phones up. She has already booked a 3.30 cut and blow-dry with Tom and wants to know if she can still come at 3.30 but have a facial as well. What would you suggest?'

Trainee's answer . . . . . .

If necessary (Yes/No) prompt: Miss L is offered a 3.30 facial with Sharon and her appointment with Tom is changed to 4.30. Mark in these appointments.

Did trainee realise implication for Mrs Z unprompted? Yes/No.

If no, prompt (Yes/No): 'Does this change affect Mrs Z's request for a perm today?'

Trainee's answer: . . . . . .

STOP THE CLOCK

(Wolf *et al*. 1990)

Allocation one: hairdressing information sheet

Two full-time stylists: Clare and
Tom   (hours 9.00 a.m. to 5.30 p.m.)
One part-time stylist: Fiona   (hours 9.30 a.m. to 2.30 p.m.)
One beauty therapist: Sharon   (hours 9.30 a.m. to 4.30 p.m.)

Appointments are being made for today.
So far:

Clare			*Tom*		
CBD	*9.00*	*Mrs. A*	*CBD*	*9.00*	*Miss G*
PERM	*9.30*	*Mrs B*	*PERM*	*9.30*	*Miss H*
PERM	*11.30*	*Mrs C*	*CBD*	*12.00*	*Miss I*
CBD	*2.00*	*Miss D*	*HI-LITE*	*1.00*	*Miss J*
PERM	*3.00*	*Mrs E*	*CBD*	*3.00*	*Mrs K*
CBD	*4.00*	*Mrs F*	*CBD*	*3.30*	*Miss L*

Fiona			*Sharon*		
CBD	*10.30*	*Ms M*	*Facial*	*12.30*	*Mrs Q*
CBD	*11.00*	*Mrs N*	*Facial*	*1.30*	*Miss R*
CBD	*11.30*	*Ms O*	*Facial*	*2.30*	*Mrs S*
CBD	*12.30*	*Mrs P*			

Appointment intervals

Allow half an hour between stylists' appointments for cut and blow-dry (CBD). These styles take one hour from start to finish.

For perms and hi-lites, allow one hour between appointments. You should then leave half an hour, and then re-book the client for a cut and blow-dry.

Allow one hour between appointments for facials, which take one hour to do.

Clients requesting a facial and a hair appointment should have the facial first. Clients should not be expected to wait more than half an hour between finishing a facial and starting their hair appointment.

Last appointments

The latest time for booking perms, hi-lites and facials is 3.30 p.m.

Fiona must leave by 2.30 p.m. at the latest to collect her toddler from playgroup. Clare and Tom may have to stay a bit later than 5.30 if they have a perm or hi-lites to finish off.

Clients should be seen by the same stylist throughout.

As these reports point out, although

> success in many occupations depends upon complex thinking
> and problem-solving skills. These processes are not measured
> directly by conventional occupational qualifications or by the
> selection processes commonly used in the field. As the 'Measur-
> ing "Broad" Skills' report emphasises, conventional assessments
> not only fail to measure thinking and problem-solving skills
> directly, but they also do not predict people's strengths in these
> areas. Both the 'Measuring "Broad" Skills' and TSAW projects
> developed innovative measures to assess thinking and problem-
> solving skills. TSAW test tasks were designed explicitly to assess
> progress over time on a range of problem-posing and problem-
> solving tactics in relation to a complex job simulation.
>   In the 'Measuring "Broad" Skills' project the two occupations
> investigated were accountancy technicians and health visitors.
>   Samples of trainees/employees were tested during their final
> qualifying year and one year into appropriate employment.
> Measures taken included: in-tray exercises; case studies; work
> samples; . . . interviews, supervisor/manager ratings of per-
> formance. . . .. Health visitors showed large improvements over
> time on case study exercises which closely reflected day to
> day working issues. . . . In contrast, ratings of performance by
> supervisors/managers were unreliable due to a high degree of
> autonomy in the job role. Accounting technicians improved
> markedly over time on the financial accounting exercise. Indi-
> viduals rated most favourably by their managers showed the
> greatest improvements.
>
> (Blagg and Lewis 1993)

Soden (1993) assessed the effect of problem-solving training on
the performance of learners pursuing modules in a range of
vocational areas. The criteria for constructing tasks to measure
problem solving were that each task should be:

1 non-routine in the sense that there are substantial elements
  which have not been present in tasks previously practised by
  the learners; and
2 capable of solution by using mental operations to manipulate
  the information prescribed for the module *or* which can be
  generated from such information by the use of mental operations
  (e.g., inference, generalisation).

Figure 7.5 shows a few of the tasks which were used to assess problem solving.

Figure 7.5 Test items from 'Teaching thinking skills in vocational education' project

Cookery processes

Suppose the following problems arose when you were cooking for a busy restaurant. What can you do to make the best of each situation?

The Victoria sponges which were for the afternoon teas have sunk in the middle.

You have made 6 lb (2.5 kilos, approx.) of pastry for apple tarts for the lunch menu. However, the pastry has turned out too crumbly and it won't roll properly.

There has been an increase in customers – from the 40 covers you expected to 60 covers.

You have been asked to cater for a party in someone's house for 30 people. The client wants some of the food to be served hot. You have to suggest the menu. What questions would you want to ask the client? What are the most likely problems?

Hairdressing: permanent waving

The perm you have just done has turned out much weaker than you wanted it to be. What would you do?

The client asked for a curly perm which was carried out correctly, but the client is disappointed at the result, saying that it is too curly. What would you do?

A client returns from holiday, her tinted hair is dry and unmanageable because of too much sun and sea water. She wants you to perm it, to make it more manageable. What would you consider your options to be? Choose up to three options.

A young client with long hair has a spiral perm which has been successfully carried out. She returns the next week with a dry, bushy, frizzy head of hair. What can you do to improve the situation?

Your client has very short, coarse, good-density hair which is proving difficult to wind. What can you do?

A client with very oily hair has had her hair softly permed. She returns in a few days to say that her hair is flat and straight. What could have gone wrong?

The perm re-agent has been poured out before the stylist is ready for it. What would you do in this situation?

Tasks which purport to measure problem-solving skills but which require only generally familiar information appear frequently in newspapers and magazines. There are examples of these tasks in Chapter 2 (the nine-dot problem) and Chapter 5 (the *Herald* Mind Game). This type of task has also been used by some researchers to measure problem-solving skills. Such tests tell us only how individuals have performed on that type of problem. They tell us very little about how they would perform on problems which require the use of occupational information. Of course, it could be argued that the instruments used in the studies reported in this chapter tell us only about the learners' problem-solving skills in the occupational areas investigated. However, this information is of more use to the person recruiting employees or selecting entrants to educational programmes in that area than information about performance on very general problems.

Evidence from task performance, such as dealing with a difficult customer, auditing accounts, writing reports or presenting information verbally to an audience, may be supplemented by other forms of evidence on assessing problem-solving skills. A dialogue between an assessor and a learner can allow the assessor to find out by posing questions whether the quality of the learner's thinking is much greater than can be revealed in the performance. Supplementary written evidence could take the form of requiring the learners to generate questions they would ask themselves in response to problems presented in a written form. It could also take the form of constructing algorithms which would work for the problems presented to the learners. Sometimes constraints will be such that the most practicable way of assessing learners' problem-solving skills is through some of these forms of written work. This does not mean that the test is flawed, but rather that what it claims to measure will be different from what other types of tests purport to measure.

In developing measures of thinking skills in vocational education it is useful to begin by establishing, through discussion with experienced practitioners, descriptions of recurring problems in a particular occupational area. A decision can then be made as to whether the assessment of the individual's problem solving is to be work-based or through a project which simulates workplace problems or whether some other activity is appropriate.

If you are keen to deepen your understanding of assessment, a paper by Alison Wolf of the University of London is well worth studying. 'Assessment issues and problems in a criterion-based system' was commissioned by the Further Education Unit as a contribution to the continuing debate over ways in which the assessment of the curriculum can be improved. The paper explores some of the uncertainties in criterion-referenced assessment systems and offers some guidance on how to deal with them. (The National Curriculum, National Vocational Qualifications and General National Vocational Qualifications have been designed to be broadly criterion-referenced.)

SUMMARY

It is a myth that transfer just happens; the road to transfer is likely to be a rocky one. People need to learn mental procedures which alert them to possibilities of using previous learning.

Assessment: decide what you want to know about trainees' problem-solving abilities and what use you will make of the information.

FURTHER READING

Blagg, N.R. and Lewis, R.E. (eds) (1993) 'A report on the development and evaluation of the Thinking Skills at Work Modules', Research Series, The Employment Dept, Moorfoot, Sheffield.

Blagg, N. R., Ballinger, M. P. and Lewis, R. (1993) Thinking skills at work (TSAW) Modules, Taunton: Nigel Blagg Associates; TSAW Preparing for Work Module; TSAW Engineering Module; TSAW Administration, Business and Commerce Module; TSAW Hotel, Catering and Licensed Trade Module.

Craig, M. (1993a) 'Fault finding and diagnosis modules', Cleveland Open Learning Unit.

—— (1993b) 'Training in fault finding and diagnosis – a systems approach: small firms' evaluation', Research Series, The Employment Dept, Moorfoot, Sheffield.

Derry, S. and Kellis, A. (1986) 'A prescriptive analysis of low-ability problem solving behaviour', Instructional Science 15: 49–65.

McGuiness, C. (1990) 'Talking about thinking: the role of meta-cognition in teaching thinking', in K.J. Gilhooly, M.T.G. Keane, R.H. Logie and G. Erdos (eds) Mines of Thinking, vol. 2, London: Wiley.

Soden, R. (1993) 'Teaching thinking skills in vocational education', Technical Report No. 13, The Employment Dept, Research and Development Series, Moorfoot, Sheffield.

Wolf, A. (1993a) 'Measuring "Broad" Skills', Research Report, Employment Dept, Moorfoot, Sheffield.

—— (1993b) 'Assessment issues and problems in a criterion based system', Further Education Unit.

Wolf, A., Fotheringham, J. and Grey, A. (1990) *Learning in Context, Research and Development*, No. 58, The Training Agency, Moorfoot, Sheffield.

Wolf, A., Silver, R. and Kelson, M. (1993) 'Learning in context', reported in N. Blagg and R. Lewis (eds) 'Thinking and learning at work', Taunton: Nigel Blagg Associates.

Chapter 8

Problem solving in kitchens

In the earlier chapters the principles of a problem-solving curriculum were explained and exemplified. Those principles are not difficult to understand. What is often difficult is the application of research in your own vocational area. This difficulty arises because researchers and practitioners have different aims: the former being concerned with extending what is known about thinking processes; and the practitioner with how to handle the next instructional session. The purpose of this chapter is to set out applications which have been developed and tried out in a number of colleges with both school leavers and adults who wanted to re-train for the catering industry. Much of the instruction and practice took place in training restaurant kitchens where lunches were prepared for guests.

A useful classification of problems in catering is (1) problems caused by errors, and (2) problems caused by changes in circumstances.

ERRORS

Many of the problems which have to be tackled in the kitchens of restaurants or institutions arise from errors. The following problems in Figure 8.1 are common ones, and are discussed on pages 140–1.

A problem-solving approach to teaching catering competences can reduce errors, and develop the ability to produce a solution which is cost-effective and maintains client satisfaction when problems do arise. When confronted with unexpected changes in requirements or resources, the caterer exposed to a problem-solving approach is more likely to produce acceptable solutions.

Figure 8.1 Errors in food preparation

Someone over-whips cream, which turns into butter, thereby creating the problem that fresh cream filling for the éclairs on the menu is not available.

The trainee chef hacks all the fresh grapefruit into pieces of a size and shape which are not considered appropriate for the grapefruit cocktail on the menu.

The trainee who is inexperienced in making bread rolls over-proves the rolls, which lose their shape and develop a lumpy texture.

An inexperienced manager offers a menu which is beyond the competences of the available staff.

In learning situations where errors occur fairly frequently, the problem-solving processes for catering can be taught through the way in which errors are dealt with. You need to go beyond a simple pointing out of the errors. It is more helpful to ask the learners to identify shortcomings in their thinking processes: these can then be remedied so that a similar type of error is less likely to arise. In the case of bread rolls being over-proved, learners can learn that they forgot to ask themselves whether the time required for proving can be predicted accurately, and what action is necessary if it cannot be predicted accurately (frequent checking is necessary).

Errors should also be used to demonstrate a problem-solving process for limiting or even eliminating the cost of the errors. For example, suppose the learners have made several kilos of pastry for apple tarts but it has turned out too crumbly and cannot be rolled out to the required size and shape. For this type of problem, identification of the cause of the problem and assessment of the degree of error can be emphasised. These are processes which have high transfer value to other types of problem, both in catering and other occupational areas. Learners can be guided towards formulation of a line of self-questioning such as that shown in Figure 8.2.

This approach to generating appropriate self-questions can be applied to most situations. Here are some of the effective self-questions that can be generated for the first two errors described in Figure 8.1 above.

Figure 8.2 Retrieving errors: crumbly pastry

What are the most probable causes of the problem? Not enough liquid or the wrong balance of ingredients has been used. What do I need to ask next to be able to answer this question?

Does the pastry bind together again if water is added? Try adding water to a small piece of the pastry. If it binds together then an egg or water can be added to the whole pastry and the problem is solved.

If the addition of liquid does not work, the problem is caused by the wrong balance of ingredients, and questions like the following need to be asked:

• Will the pastry have a satisfactory taste when it is baked?
• How much do I need to bake to find out?
• How much time do I have? (If time is short try it in the microwave.) If it bakes satisfactorily, consider alternative uses compatible with the fact that apples have already been prepared (apple crumble).
• If the pastry is not suitable for a crumble dish, are there other alternative uses for the pastry?
• If it cannot be rolled out, what small items could be made from the pastry? (e.g., Empire biscuits).

---

1 Where the learner over-whipped the cream for the chocolate éclair filling and no more fresh cream was available, the following questions would have moved the learner towards an acceptable solution:

(a) What other kinds of filling are appropriate for the chocolate éclairs?
Synthetic cream? – Do we have a supply? If not, then:
(b) Make pastry cream? What are the ingredients and do we have them? Is there enough time to make it (fast preparation time but takes time to cool)? How can I cool it quickly?
(c) How can any food or liquid be cooled more quickly (split into smaller amounts? set it on something cold such as water and ice in a bain-marie)?

2 The following line of self-questioning would have helped the trainee chef who found himself with insufficient grapefruit segments for the grapefruit cocktail because he had not managed to use the knives properly:

(a) What kind of solutions are there to a shortage problem?
(b) Have I had a shortage problem before (e.g., carrots were burned, potatoes were left too long to boil)? (Solutions were based on bulking or concealing the error.)
What were the main features of bulking and concealing (e.g., adding a compatible ingredient such as adding frozen carrots to the insufficient fresh carrots, serving peas as well as carrots, adding powdered potato)? Would it be helpful to change the grapefruit into another form?
(c) What is the main feature of transforming food (changing it by mashing, liquidising, etc. – e.g. mashing over-boiled potatoes)? Is liquidising a good solution? (No – there's plenty of juice in stock if this is acceptable as an alternative.)
(d) Can ingredients be added to make the grapefruit go further? Do we have these ingredients (tinned or fresh citrus fruit)?
(e) Concealment? (Hacked up pieces can go in the bottom of a glass, covered by the proper sized pieces and some tinned fruit.)

The following problems illustrate how the same basic self-questions are effective for dealing with a variety of problems. The approach therefore has high transfer value.

A common problem is that a cake such as a Victoria sponge fails to rise. Learners who had mastered this problem-solving approach might pursue the following self-questions.

1 How much time do I have?
2 Is the outer ring of the sponge of good quality? (If so, fill it with fruit and cream.)
3 If there is no cream, have I time to make an alternative filling (e.g., pastry cream)?
4 If it is not of good quality could it be crumbed and made into sweets? (What kind of sweets can be made from cake crumbs in the time available, e.g., trifles?)

Problem-solving skill can be developed by helping learners to generate appropriate questions for tackling various types of situation. For example, in planning menus for the employees of a company the following would be appropriate questions:

1 Has the company specified that the catering operation is to break even, produce a profit or be given a subsidy?
2 What proportion of the employees are doing heavy manual

work? What proportion are mainly doing desk work? Numbers of males and females?

3 Are there constraints arising from religious and other beliefs? Are there other known preferences, e.g., plain Scottish food, foreign dishes?

4 What competences do the kitchen staff possess?

5 What constraints are imposed by equipment or storage space, delivery times?

Time should be set aside for discussing problems which arise from unexpected changes.

A restaurant training manager used the common problem of an unexpected increase in customers – say, from forty to sixty – to guide the group of learners towards formulating a set of questions:

1 Which dishes on the menu can be expanded easily without loss of quality – and how? (For instance, soup could be bulked by the addition of some packet soup mix.)

2 What scope is there for reducing the portion size of some items and compensating by substitution of others which can be made very quickly? (For example, reduce apple tart, increase custard.)

3 What extra dishes could be prepared quickly? (For instance, ice cream, chocolate sauce, tinned fruit.)

4 How can we make some of the portions appear larger than they are?

Some problems are caused mainly by changes which the chefs could not reasonably have foreseen. These would include power cuts or reductions in power at some point in the cookery process. A mini case study of a chef in a factory canteen faced with an unexpected electricity power cut an hour before meals are due to be served is the kind of problem that may be presented to learners. This provides practice in solving problems beyond the ones which occur naturally in the learning situation. A set of questions would be developed by the training manager leading his or her learners.

1 How can I find out the likely duration of this power cut and whether neighbouring companies are also affected?

2 Will the time interval contravene hygiene regulations? If so, then:
   How much spare capacity is there in our gas cookers? If not sufficient, then:
   Have neighbouring establishments enough spare capacity they are willing to lend?

If not:
Ask management if workers can have an early lunch.

The following set of questions are applicable to most cooking tasks. The use of these self-questions should become so automatic that cooks are scarcely aware that they are thinking as well as doing.

1 What type of food am I cooking, and what do I know about it? (e.g., meat; tough, tender; vegetables; grown above or below ground)
2 What process applies and what do I know about it? (e.g., sauté – temperature – coating)
3 What equipment?
4 Cooking time?
5 What preparation?
6 Order of work (e.g., which items take the longest to cook)?
7 How will I know when it is cooked?
8 Does it need a garnish?
9 How is it presented? (e.g., liquidise soup; sieve potatoes)

This chapter was developed in collaboration with Caroline McCallum, a lecturer in the Catering Department at Ayr College, Scotland.

FURTHER READING

Blagg, N. R. and Lewis, R. E. (eds) (1993) 'A report on the development and evaluation of the Thinking Skills at Work Modules', Research Series, The Employment Dept, Moorfoot, Sheffield.
Blagg, N.R., Ballinger, M.P. and Lewis, R. (1993) 'Thinking Skills at Work (TSAW) Modules', Taunton: Nigel Blagg Associates: TSAW Preparing for Work Module; TSAW Engineering Module; TSAW Administration, Business and Commerce Module; TSAW Hotel, Catering and Licensed Trade Module.
Craig, M. (1993a) 'Fault finding and diagnosis modules', Cleveland Open Learning Unit.
—— (1993b) 'Training in fault finding and diagnosis – a systems approach: small firms' evaluation', Research Series, The Employment Dept, Moorfoot, Sheffield.
Derry, S. and Kellis, A. (1986) 'A prescriptive analysis of low-ability problem solving behaviour', *Instructional Science* 15: 49–65.
Francis, H. (1991) *Individuality in Learning*, London: Further Education Unit.
Glaser, R. (1984) 'Education and thinking: the role of knowledge', *American Psychologist* 39: 93–104.

Greene, J. (1987) *Concepts and Schemata*, London: Cassell.

Landa, L. N. (1974) *Algorithmization in Learning and Instruction Publications*, Englewood Cliffs, NJ: Educational Technology Publications.

—— (1976) *Instructional Regulation and Control*, Englewood Cliffs, NJ: Educational Technology Publications.

—— (1984) 'How do we teach novices to perform at expert level?' *Contemporary Educational Psychology* 9(3): 235–45.

Lerner, I.Y.A. (1980) *The Process of Instruction and its Laws*, Moscow: Znanie.

McGuiness, C. (1990) 'Talking about thinking: the role of metacognition in teaching thinking', in K.J. Gilhooly, M.T.G. Keane, R.H. Logie and G. Erdos (eds) *Mines of Thinking*, vol. 2, London: Wiley.

McGuiness, C. and Nisbet, J. (1991) 'Teaching thinking in Europe', *British Journal of Educational Psychology* 61: 174–85.

Nisbet, J. and Shucksmith, J. (1986) *Learning Strategies*, London: Routledge.

Reigeluth, C.M. (1987) *Instructional Theories in Action*, Hillsdale, NJ: Lawrence Erlbaum.

Smith, L. (1986) 'Ability learning: an analysis of Piaget's theory of ability in adolescence', London: Further Education Unit Occasional Paper, Longman.

Wolf. A. (1993a) 'Measuring "Broad" Skills', Research Report, The Employment Dept, Moorfoot, Sheffield.

—— (1993b) 'Assessment issues and problems in a criterion based system, London: Further Education Unit.

Wolf, A., Fotheringham, J. and Grey, A. (1990) *Learning in Context, Research and Development*, No. 58, The Training Agency, Moorfoot, Sheffield.

Wolf, A., Silver, R. and Kelson, M. (1993) 'Learning in context', reported in N. Blagg and R. Lewis (eds) 'Thinking and learning at work', Taunton: Nigel Blagg Associates.

Chapter 9

Problem solving in sequential logic, transposition of formulae, applied chemistry and cardio-pulmonary resuscitation

SEQUENTIAL LOGIC MODULES

This section describes how the approach was put into practice by Russell McAllister, a lecturer at Motherwell College.

At the beginning of these modules the typical problems are relatively simple ones which many learners can solve without any great difficulty. It is easy to understand why you might think that it is unnecessary to highlight the thinking processes involved when the learners' answers suggest that their thinking is on the right lines.

However, making these processes visible to learners at this stage helps them to gain insight into the nature of thinking and enables them to become fairly skilled in constructing thinking procedures for themselves, before they are faced with more complex problems.

In the first week of a level 2 module on sequential logic the tutor presented the following problem in Figure 9.1:

Figure 9.1 Sequential logic problem (1)

when A = '1' the caller's handset is on the rest;
when B = '1' the correct number is dialled;
when C = '1' the receiver's handset is on the rest.

Let P = '1' for the connection to be made.

1 Derive the truth table, and
2 the Boolean expression;
3 draw the logic circuit using AND, OR, NOT gates.

The learners, whose ages ranged from sixteen to forty, were invited to try to solve the problem, working in small groups. After about 10 minutes, when most of the learners were asking for help from the lecturer, he posed the following questions and noted learners' answers on the chalkboard. (An example of how Russell McAllister modelled (that is, talked aloud) the type of questions which would lead to the construction of a rational procedure – namely, an algorithm – is shown in Figure 9.2.)

Figure 9.2 Sequential logic problem (1) – modelling mental operations

What are we looking for when we read the problem? (inputs and outputs)
    How many *inputs*? (3)
    How many *input combinations*? (8)
Are the inputs labelled or do you have to label them? (labelled A, B, C)
    How many outputs? (. . .)
    Are they labelled? (P)
What does a truth table contain? (inputs and outputs)
Complete the Truth table

	Truth Table			
	Inputs A B C			*Outputs*
0				
1				
2				
3				
4				
5				
6				
7				

What has to be worked out next? (where we are going to get an output?)
Is there an output from the first line?
Why/why not?
(The Why/why not question was applied to each line.)
How many outputs? (1)
∴ P = A, B, C.

A second problem was presented.

Figure 9.3 Sequential logic problem (2)

In a chemical process an alarm buzzer sounds if the temperature rises above a specified level, if the pressure rises above a specified level or the supply of raw materials is not above a specified minimum.

Devise truth table
Boolean expression
Draw the AND, OR, NOT gate circuit.

As in the first problem, learners were asked to try to tackle the problem, working in small groups, for about 10 minutes. As before, the lecturer then modelled the type of self-questions for this class of problem and wrote the learners' responses on the chalkboard.

Figure 9.4 Modelling mental operations for problem in Figure 9.3.

What are we looking for when we read the problem? (inputs)
How many inputs? (3)
Are they labelled? (No)
What labels could be used? (T, P, R)
How many outputs? (1)
What is it? (buzzer): label B
Construct the Truth table:

T	P	R	B

How many 1s? (7)
Which line has only 1? (B)
What is B (. . .)
How can we get B back to B?

When a set of questions had been agreed they were noted by the learners, who then applied them to other problems of this type.

Throughout this module, the learners were involved in contributing to the construction or modification of algorithms. In his modelling of questions which needed to be asked, the lecturer constantly emphasised how previously learned knowledge could be brought to bear on the current problem. By questioning, they came to realise how their past knowledge of NAND gates could be used to analyse the S-R Bistable. Questions posed by the lecturer provided a model for the learners of how they could interrogate their existing knowledge to build up a procedure for a new problem.

Learners were encouraged not only to test and modify algorithms which had been built up with the lecturer but also to construct, test and adapt their own algorithm for each type of problem they encountered during the module. Thus construction

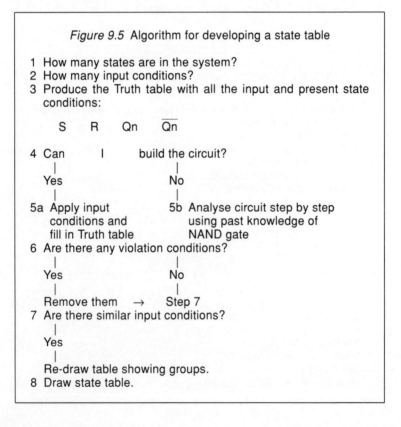

Figure 9.5 Algorithm for developing a state table

1 How many states are in the system?
2 How many input conditions?
3 Produce the Truth table with all the input and present state conditions:

    S   R   Qn $\overline{Qn}$

4 Can   I   build the circuit?
    | |
    Yes   No
    | |
5a Apply input   5b Analyse circuit step by step
    conditions and   using past knowledge of
    fill in Truth table   NAND gate
6 Are there any violation conditions?
    | |
    Yes   No
    | |
    Remove them   →   Step 7
7 Are there similar input conditions?
    |
    Yes
    |
    Re-draw table showing groups.
8 Draw state table.

of algorithms by learners was built into all the work of the module. Figure 9.5 shows an algorithm which was developed with the learners in the way outlined above.

PROBLEMS INVOLVING TRANSPOSITION OF FORMULAE

The material in this section was developed by Martin Macdonald, a lecturer in Glasgow's newest university, Glasgow Caledonian.

The lecturer who developed the algorithm in this section reported that over the years, problems which require transpositions of formulae cause never-ending problems for engineering and construction learners.

Although transpositions are also part of the GCSE syllabuses and their Scottish counterparts, many entrants to courses in engineering and construction are handicapped by their lack of competence in this procedure. Since problems involving transpositions have to be solved frequently in engineering and construction jobs it is well worth remedying the deficiency.

Martin Macdonald first developed algorithms to guide the thinking of learners who had left school with poor achievements in mathematics. However, when he was teaching learners with university entrance qualifications in mathematics, he found that the algorithm approach was still valued by the learners for its explicitness. Learners were more quickly able to handle engineering problems when algorithms had been built up to guide their thinking. Figure 9.6 shows examples of transposition problems which learners often find difficult to solve.

The algorithm in Figure 9.7 which Martin Macdonald used is powerful enough to deal with a range of problems involving transposition of formulae.

As noted in earlier chapters, it is useful, if time permits at the beginning of a programme, to introduce the idea of expressing in algorithmic form the thinking required to solve problems by building up with the learners an algorithm for an everyday problem – for example, how to get to work if there is a bus or rail strike.

As noted throughout this book, although the algorithm itself is important, representing as it does an efficient way of thinking about a type of problem, the way it is introduced to learners is at least as important. The following steps are intended not only to

Figure 9.6 Transposition problems and solutions, demonstrating the use of the algorithm to learners

(2) $F = \dfrac{mv^2}{r}$ (v)

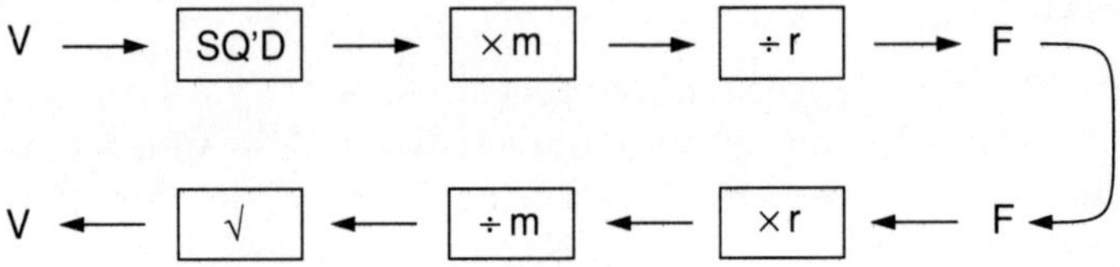

i.e. $v = \sqrt{\dfrac{Fr}{m}}$

(3) $A = \Pi r (r + 2h)$ (h)

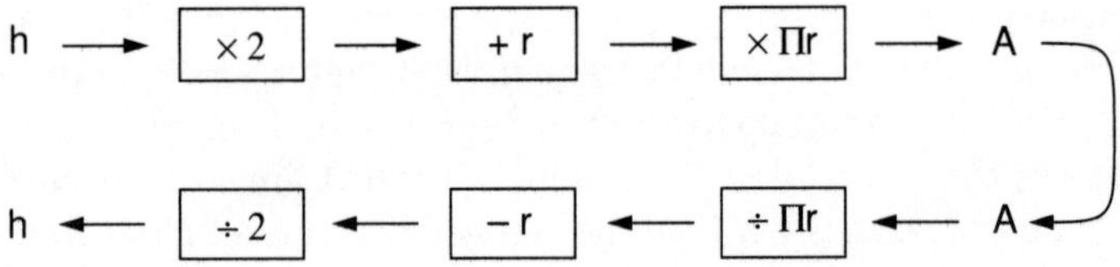

i.e. $h = \dfrac{\dfrac{A}{\Pi r} - r}{2} = \dfrac{A}{2\Pi r} - \dfrac{r}{2} = \dfrac{A - r(\Pi r)}{2\Pi r}$

or $h = \dfrac{A - \Pi r^2}{2\Pi r}$

(6) $C = \dfrac{N - n}{2p}$ (n)

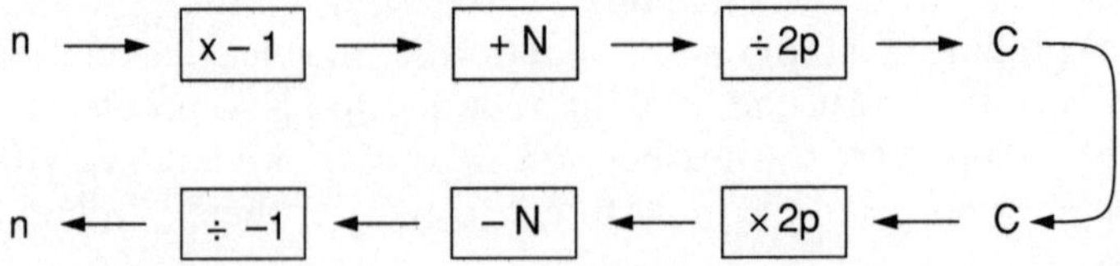

i.e. $n = \dfrac{2pC - N}{-1}$ i.e. $n = -2pC + N$

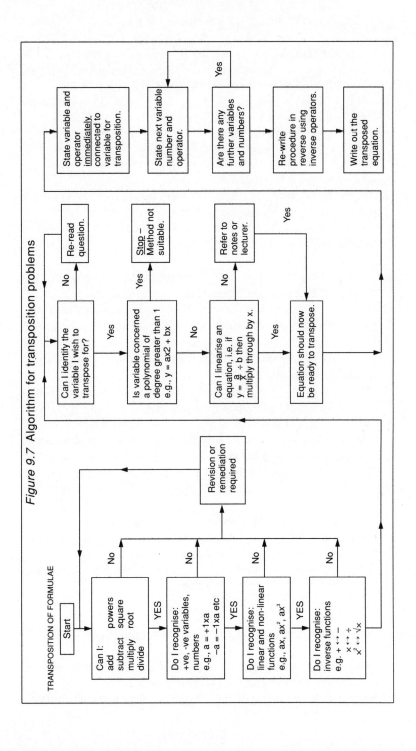

Figure 9.7 Algorithm for transposition problems

instruct learners in how to use the algorithm, but the aim is also to develop an understanding of how they themselves can construct a rational plan in the form of an algorithm. These steps should be read in conjunction with the transposition problems and their solutions shown in Figure 9.6.

1 If you have not done so already, explain to learners what is meant by mental operations, using simple mathematical examples: e.g., addition and subtraction.

2 Revise by questioning the relevant mathematical symbols, powers and trigonometric functions.

Revise by questioning that, when we write '2 A', it means 'A multiplied by +2'; i.e., +2 × A, when we write '−A' the meaning is −1 × A . . . and so on.

Revise by questioning that if we add the inverse is subtract; if we square the inverse is the square root; and so on.

3 Using the examples in Figure 9.6, show on an overhead projector (OHP) the first column only of the algorithm in Figure 9.7 which reminds learners what they must know if they are to be successful at transposition of formulae and, if necessary, to remediate gaps in their knowledge.

4 Introduce mental operations of searching for an equation of a similar type to the one presented (e.g., $T/J = \tau/r$ is a very similar equation to $M/I = \sigma/y$; $F = ma$ is a very similar equation to $V = IR$). Demonstrate, using examples, that the transposition steps will be similar for most equations of the same type. Point out that the search can be helped by asking oneself the question 'What is the main feature of this equation?' Try out this question on examples.

5 Discuss with learners questions they could ask themselves to get started. Write suggestions on board/chart. If questions suggested do not include the most useful ones, demonstrate with examples why they are not as useful as other questions. Show on an OHP *second* column of the algorithm in Figure 9.7. Apply the questioning to an example, asking learners to supply answers.

Ask if learners can suggest more useful questions.

6 Ask learners to suggest questions to progress the transposition. Deal with suggestions as in 5 above. Show on an OHP the *third* column of the flow-chart. Continue as in 5 above.

7 Issue copies of the algorithm (Figure 9.7) to learners together

Figure 9.8 Transposition problems and solutions

(1)   v = u + at   (t)

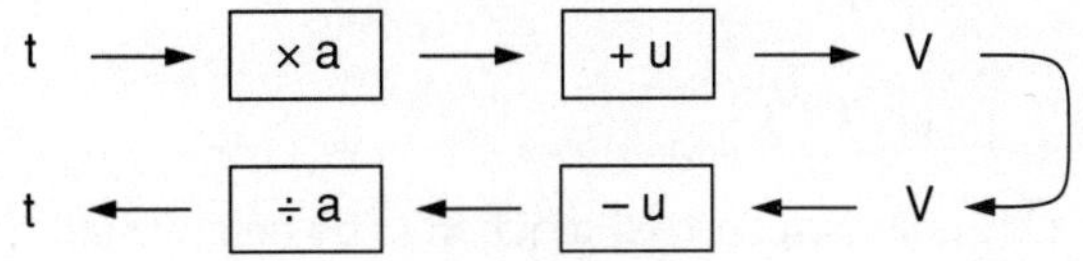

t ⟶ | × a | ⟶ | + u | ⟶ V ⤵

t ⟵ | ÷ a | ⟵ | − u | ⟵ V ⟵

i.e., $t = \dfrac{v - u}{a}$

---

(4) $X = \dfrac{1}{2\pi fc}$ (c)

Linearise: X2πfc = 1

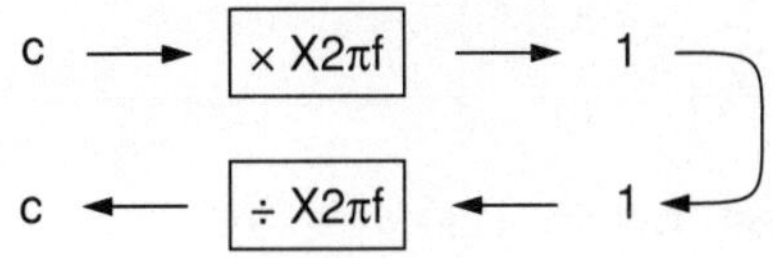

c ⟶ | × X2πf | ⟶ 1 ⤵

c ⟵ | ÷ X2πf | ⟵ 1 ⟵

i.e., $c = \dfrac{1}{x\pi f}$

---

(5) $\dfrac{M}{I} = \dfrac{\sigma}{y}$ (y)

Linearise: $\dfrac{My}{I} = \sigma$

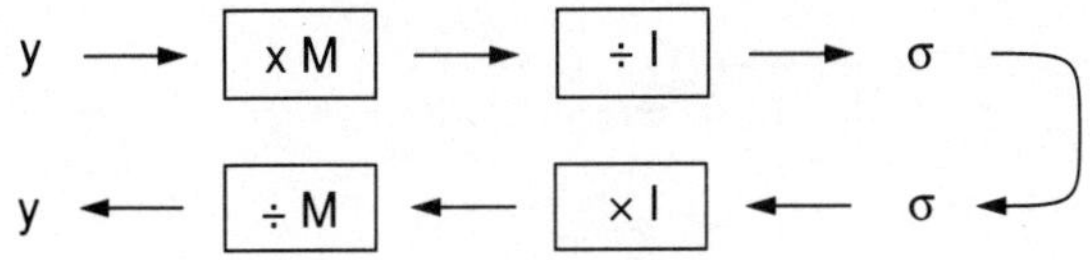

y ⟶ | × M | ⟶ | ÷ I | ⟶ σ ⤵

y ⟵ | ÷ M | ⟵ | × I | ⟵ σ ⟵

i.e., $y = \dfrac{\sigma I}{M}$

The following is an example of a more advanced type of problem which is often difficult for learners and for which the algorithm in Figure 9.7 also provides guidance.

A hollow shaft of 200 mm outside diameter and 100 mm inside diameter is used to transmit power with a torque rating of 73.63 kNm. Determine the angle of twist in radians per unit length of shaft. Take the modules of rigidity to be 80 GNm^{-2}.

Figure 9.9 Solution for the 'hollow shaft' problem

Theory of Torsion states:

$$\frac{T}{J} = \frac{\tilde{i}}{r} = \frac{G\theta}{\ell}$$

Since $\tilde{i}$ is unknown and not required to be determined the theory reduces to

$$\frac{T}{J} = \frac{G\theta}{\ell} \qquad \text{hence from specification}$$

$$T = 73.63 \text{ kNm} = 73.63 \times 10^3 \text{ Nm}$$

$$J = \frac{\pi}{32}(D^4 - d^4) \qquad \text{where D } 0.2 \text{ m and } d = 01.\text{ m}$$

$$J = \frac{\pi}{32}(0.2^4 - 0.1^4)$$

$$\therefore J = 0.147 \times 10^{-3} \text{ m}^4$$

$$G = 80 \text{ GNm}^{-2} = 80 \times 10^9 \text{ Nm}^{-2}$$

$$\ell = 1 \text{ m} \qquad \theta = ? \text{ radian.}$$

Using algorithm to transpose equation for θ

$$\frac{T}{J} = \frac{G\theta}{\ell} \qquad (\theta)$$

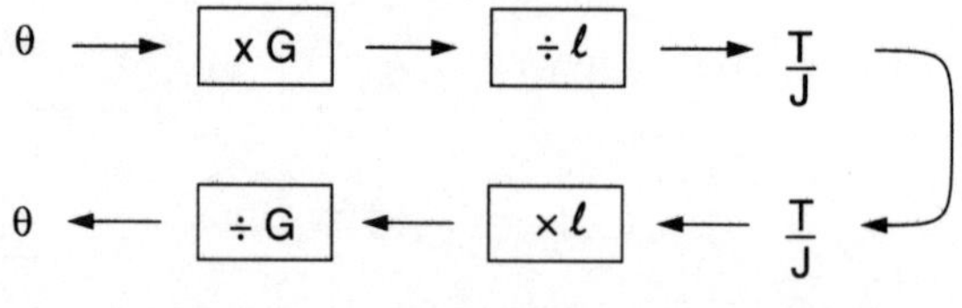

$$\theta \longrightarrow \boxed{\times G} \longrightarrow \boxed{\div \ell} \longrightarrow \frac{T}{J}$$

$$\theta \longleftarrow \boxed{\div G} \longleftarrow \boxed{\times \ell} \longleftarrow \frac{T}{J}$$

$$\text{i.e., } \theta = \frac{T}{J} \times \frac{\ell}{G}$$

Using information

$$\theta = \frac{73.63 \times 10^3 \times 1}{0.147 \times 10^{-3} \times 80 \times 10^9} = 0.00625 \text{ radian}$$

$$\text{or } \theta = \frac{0.00625 \times 180}{\pi} \qquad \begin{array}{l} - \text{ compare to degree} \\ \text{equivalent} \end{array}$$

$$= 0.36° \text{ of twist per metre length of shaft}$$

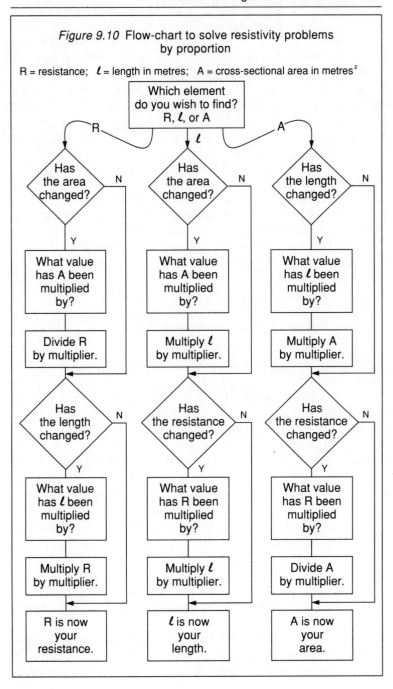

Figure 9.10 Flow-chart to solve resistivity problems by proportion

R = resistance; ℓ = length in metres;   A = cross-sectional area in metres^2

with items 1, 4 and 5 in Figure 9.8. Ask learners to tick each question in the algorithm as they provide the answer and carry out the step. (For the reader's convenience the solutions for items 1, 4 and 5 also appear in Figure 9.8. Obviously, the solutions would not be issued to learners at this point.)

8 Provide feedback. If learners are having difficulty with any of the problems, ask them to talk you through the algorithm. They may have had difficulty in answering some of the questions in the algorithm or they may have missed steps.

The flow-chart in Figure 9.10 was developed by lecturers in Aberdeen, Motherwell and Falkirk Colleges.

Resistivity problems in electrical engineering are an example of a type of problem which is difficult for some students at NVQ level 2 because they are unable to carry out the necessary manipulation of the formula $R = \frac{\rho l}{a}$ where R is resistance, ρ is resistivity, l is length and a is area. Many learners fail to make progress with, for instance, the topic mutual and self-inductance because they are confused about handling the formula. Figure 9.10 on page 155 provides a thinking guide for such calculations.

ORGANIC CHEMISTRY: AROMATIC SYNTHESIS

Figure 9.11 was developed by Dr Jemima Magna, a lecturer at Fife College of Technology.

Many of the learners who want to achieve an HNC/HND in organic chemistry find organic synthesis extremely difficult to master. The main problem is not the understanding of the individual steps once deduced, but rather the derivation of these steps in the correct sequence. In an attempt to improve learner performance Magna (1990), helped learners to devise a series of questions (Figure 9.11) which, she hypothesised, would allow them to access the relevant concept structures in a way which would increase the probability of a correct solution. (The importance of concept structures in problem solving is discussed in Chapter 3.) It should be emphasised that this guided discovery of a series of questions to improve retrieval of concepts was undertaken only after she had checked, through administration of a test, that the learners had actually acquired satisfactory concept structures relating to aromatic synthesis. Thus, in summary, what Magna is positing is that the difficulty the learners have is not in

Figure 9.11 Self-questions in organic chemistry

Aromatic synthesis

Is the substitution

A SIDE-CHAIN?

   Is it   NUCLEOPHILIC   or   RADICAL?
           which nucleophile?   which radical?
           which reactant?   which reactant?

B RING?

   ELECTROPHILIC?
   • Which groups are to be inserted?
   • Are these formed from other groups?
   • What is the directive influence of each group?
   • What is the required orientation of the groups
     in the product?
   • Which group must be inserted first?
   • Which group next, etc.?
   • Is there a choice? Then consider the activating
     influence of each group – most activating
     takes priority.
   • Decide final order of insertion.
   • Write reaction scheme.
   • State reagents for each step.

Group	Pre-group	Directive influence	Required orientation	Activating influence	order

Reaction scheme:

acquiring the concept structures but in bringing them to bear on problems. (See the appendix for a summary of research in other vocational areas which tried to improve application of knowledge.)

Magna's overall aim was to develop the learners' insight into the nature of problem solving in organic chemistry, so that they would be able to devise their own series of questions for future synthesis problems in different topic areas. She predicted that this ability to generate their own questions would improve the speed and efficiency of their practical work.

It is worth noting that Magna, after the guided discovery of the series of question in Figure 9.11, took steps to ensure that learners actually used the questions in working out practice problems. Magna supervised the practice, checking that the learners were asking themselves each of the questions in Figure 9.11 and recording their answers in the table at the bottom of Figure 9.11.

Magna's preliminary results are very encouraging. She administered two problem-solving tests both to her experimental group, who were exposed to the new approach, and to her control group, who were not exposed to the approach. The first test was administered before the experimental group was exposed to the guided discovery session which led to the compilation and use of the questions in Figure 9.11.

Both groups practised solving problems after the first test. The experimental group used the questions in Figure 9.11, but the control group did not refer to any list of questions. In the second test, following the practice, the experimental group achieved significantly higher scores than in the first test, whereas the control group's scores did not improve. When the experimental group's scores were compared with those of previous classes, the increase is substantially greater than that achieved by the previous students over a similar period of practice. Magna intends to carry out more tightly controlled, larger-scale studies in the future to find out whether these promising results from this pilot study can be replicated.

CARDIO-PULMONARY RESUSCITATION

The materials in this section were developed by Lynn Wallace, a clinical supervisor in Queen Margaret College, Edinburgh.

The task of cardio-pulmonary resuscitation (CPR) in basic life support is a vital life-saving skill for student nurses to acquire.

Research indicates poor acquisition and retention of CPR skills among nurses. In one study, only 20 per cent of third-year student nurses achieved competence. Other research findings suggest that time practising may not be the most important factor in learning CPR. Baccalaureate student nurses continued to demonstrate poor levels of competence following extensive opportunity to practise. Student nurses' scores on retention of knowledge tests did not correlate with competence. CPR information was retained, but student nurses were unable to apply this knowledge satisfactorily.

It could be suggested that although practising the physical movements is necessary in CPR learning, rehearsal of thinking procedures is at least as important to successful application. The teaching methods currently employed by most nurse tutors include information giving, using a combination of video, lecture-discussion, teacher demonstration and student practice sessions but not explicit rehearsal of thinking procedures.

Since the instructional techniques noted above had not led to a satisfactory outcome it was decided to add to these techniques guided discovery and use of an algorithm (Figure 9.12) that guides the student nurses through a thinking procedure which is efficient for this task. The immediate benefit expected from this addition is that the student nurses will learn a sequence of questions which will improve their recall of the steps required for the performance of cardio-pulmonary resuscitation. Although recalling the steps required to apply information to a practical task is not the same as actually carrying out the task, it is a significant step in the right direction. In the longer run, if this approach is continued in other classes, the student nurses may enhance their insight into the nature of knowledge and its application.

Wallace (1993) carried out an initial test of her hypothesis with two groups of undergraduates. There were sixteen undergraduates in the experimental group and nineteen in the control group. Both groups watched a video demonstration of CPR supported by relevant information. Both groups then received a handout summarising the important points which had been covered. The control group were exposed to a tutor-led discussion on the handout, which was intended to promote revision and to provide an opportunity to raise questions. This discussion was not carried out with the experimental group. Instead, an incomplete CPR algorithm was issued to this group. Discussion of the algorithm was designed to promote the students' understanding

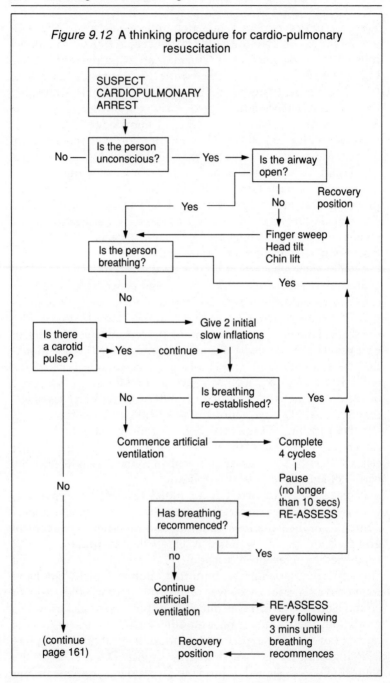

Figure 9.12 A thinking procedure for cardio-pulmonary resuscitation

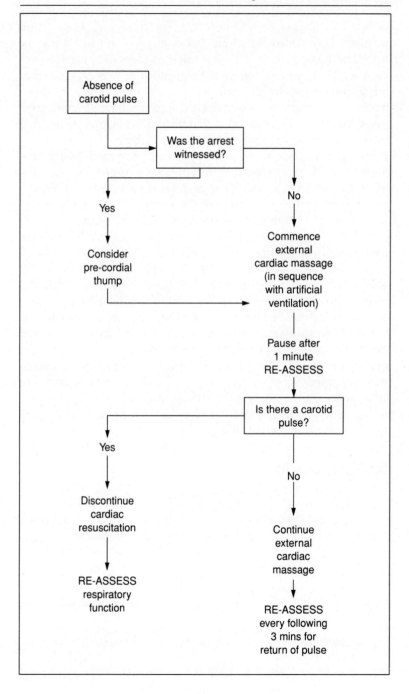

of how a sequence of questions can be developed. Each group member read out to the group either a question (decision to be made) or the response to the question (processes to be carried out). Figure 9.12 shows the completed algorithm. It was expected that this approach would also help the learners to structure the information in memory in a way which would facilitate its application (see Chapter 3). It was planned that directional arrows be inserted by the learners as the sequence of the algorithm was followed.

Both groups then had equal opportunity to practise CPR on a manikin, each group being supervised by a tutor who provided feedback. Feedback was provided also by peers and by the manikin computer/recorder. A diagrammatic handout was issued at the beginning of the practice period to help the learners to recall the positioning in order to resuscitate the patient. The learners were assessed by a practical test on a manikin (Objective Structured Clinical Assessment – OSCE). The experimental group attained 10 per cent greater achievement of competence than the control group on this test. However, this small difference probably underestimates the benefit of the algorithm, since it was not possible to match the groups with regard to age and past experience. In the experimental group, fewer learners had previous experience of CPR than in the group with which performance was compared. This research is being continued and extended to other areas of the undergraduate programme.

The materials in this chapter were developed in collaboration with lecturers in Scottish colleges.

FURTHER READING

Assink, E.M. (1987) 'Algorithms in spelling instruction: the orthography of Dutch verbs', *Journal of Educational Psychology* 79 (3): 228–35.

Landa, L.N. (1974) *Algorithmization in Learning and Instruction Publications*, Englewood Cliffs, NJ: Educational Technology Publications.

—— (1976) *Instructional Regulation and Control*, Englewood Cliffs, NJ: Educational Technology Publications.

—— (1984) 'How do we teach novices to perform at expert level? *Contemporary Educational Psychology* 9 (3): 235–45.

Mayer, R. E. (1983) *Thinking, Problem Solving, Cognition*, New York: W. H. Freeman.

Mettes, C., Pilot, A. and Roosink, H.J. (1981) 'Linking factual and procedural knowledge in solving science problems', *Instructional Science* 10 (4): 333–61.

Terlouw, C. and Mettes, C.T. (1984) 'A systematic problem approach for designing policy: validation by experts and tudents', Doc 84–12, Educational Centre, University of Twente.

REFERENCES

Magna, J. (1990) 'Teaching problem solving in HND organic chemistry', Unpublished dissertation, Scottish School of Further Education, University of Strathclyde.

Wallace, L. (1993) 'Problem solving and the application of a learning algorithm as a means of effective instruction in cardio-pulmonary resuscitation', Unpublished dissertation, Scottish School of Further Education, University of Strathclyde.

Chapter 10

A problem-solving approach in basic principles of accounting

Many learners never achieve a clear understanding of the principles of double entry bookkeeping and the preparation of simple final accounts. They rely on remembering that accounts like rent and heating usually have debit entries, while entries in others like sales are usually made on the credit side, and that final accounts can be drawn up by memorising the items in previous examples. Reliance on this rote approach seriously hinders progress, thereby reducing interest, motivation and ability to proceed with what is an important part of a business studies programme.

The psychological explanations of learning and problem solving set out in the previous chapters shed considerable light on these difficulties, and suggest how learners can be helped towards an understanding of the principles of accounting. It was noted that understanding comes from knowing the relationships between the different concepts which make up an area of knowledge and knowing the relationships between these concepts and other knowledge of an everyday nature. For example, the task in Figure 10.1 requires knowledge of the relationship between purchases, sales, stock and profit.

RESULTS FROM EXPERIMENTAL INSTRUCTIONAL MATERIALS

The examples in this section of learning materials are part of a set of materials which were designed to help learners to establish the relationship between accounting concepts, and to help them to develop efficient mental procedures for applying the knowledge. The complete set of materials was used in an experiment, which compared the performance of fifty further education students

Figure 10.1 Relationship between basic concepts

A shopkeeper gives you the following information about the business at the end of its trading year.

	£000s
Its *sales* for the year were	50
Its *purchases* of goods for the year were	30
When the year *began* it had a *stock of goods* valued at	5
At the *end* of the year it has a *stock of goods* valued at	10

(a) What was its gross profit for this year?
(b) Its total expenses (e.g., heating, insurance) incurred during the year in earning this profit were £5,000.

What effect would these expenses have on the gross profit (please tick appropriate box below)?

(a) Increase the gross profit?
(b) Decrease the gross profit?
(c) Have no effect on the gross profit?

who were exposed to these materials with that of a control group who did not use these materials, but instead were supplied with the learning materials normally used by their tutors. The experimental and control groups were matched on relevant variables. Both groups had enrolled for the forty-hour SCOTVEC module, Financial Record Keeping. Both groups of students were continuously assessed on the SCOTVEC learning outcomes for this module, and in addition both groups were tested on problems based on the SCOTVEC learning outcomes. The experimental group who had been exposed to this set of learning materials outperformed the control group, and the difference in performance was statistically and educationally significant (Soden 1990).

FEATURES OF THE EXPERIMENTAL MATERIALS

Two important purposes of financial record-keeping are kept before the students from the beginning of the module. These purposes are to find out if the business

1 is making a profit or a loss – and how much;
2 can meet its debts as they fall due.

The concepts of profit, assets and liabilities are not covered by the outcomes for this module, yet these are central ideas in accounting which give meaning to the more subordinate concepts that are included in this module. The concepts of purchases and sales are more meaningful when the concept of profit is taught. The significance of debtors, creditors, overdrafts and so on is easier to understand if these concepts are related to the more general ones such as assets, liabilities and solvency of the business. This gain in meaningfulness can be achieved without going into more detailed description of these more general concepts. An elementary understanding of these concepts will enhance the meaning of the more subordinate ones introduced in the module and help students to build a framework into which all accounting concepts can be fitted. For example, the task in Figure 10.1 does not require a detailed knowledge of final accounts, but makes the student think about the connections between profit and purchases, sales and stock.

In the first ten hours of the module, students work on materials designed to promote understanding of important accounting concepts before they are introduced to daybooks, ledger entries or, indeed, any formal accounting statement. When students are introduced right from the beginning to any formal accounting statement, such as ledger accounts or balance sheets, they often restrict their attention to copying a layout rather than pursuing understanding of the underlying principle. This tendency has also been reported in the learning of other subjects such as statistics and arithmetic, when procedures are introduced before the reality which the procedure represents is understood.

It is easy to see examples of this lack of understanding in young children's learning of multiplication tables. If they have not had sufficient practice in manipulating concrete materials, the tables are learned in a rote way which is boring and takes longer than understanding-based learning. Children learn better what multiplication means if they are encouraged to arrange objects into a row (of, say, 6) and to add on rows so that they can check for themselves that 7 rows of 6 objects make a total of 42 objects. The experimental materials for double-entry bookkeeping are designed to induce understanding of the everyday reality behind

ledger entries. However, although children usually need to manipulate physical objects to achieve understanding, adults and older
secondary school students can achieve understanding through
verbal descriptions of reality. In the experimental materials, by the
time the students are introduced to the ledger they will understand that every transaction has two effects on a business. They
will be able to describe, in accounting language, the effects of all
the transactions they will encounter; for example, that a payment
to a creditor results in a decrease in creditors, which causes a
reduction in total indebtedness of the business and a decrease in
cash at bank.

Throughout the materials, the exercises are designed to promote understanding of the connection between daybooks, ledger
and final accounts. This tying together of knowledge, as noted
throughout the book, helps to produce transferable use of knowledge. The need to form in the student's mind the correct sequences of mental operations required for any task is also
emphasised. The experimental materials contain algorithms for
the major bookkeeping tasks.

The instructional materials (set 1) show how this approach
is applied to developing understanding of the relationship
between purchases, sales, gross profit, cash, debtors and creditors. Earlier in the materials, the concepts of purchases, sales,
gross profit and cash are introduced, and the distinctions between cash and credit and between cash and bank transactions
are made in a section of the materials which is not reproduced
here. A fuller explanation of capital also appears in materials
which are not reproduced here. (Capital is explained as having
the features of a loan from the owner to the business.) Note
that no ledger entries or final accounts are drawn up at
this point.

The instructional materials are designed either for independent
learning or for conventional 'lessons'. The complete set of materials
forms an explanatory script (plus activities) which can take the
place of tutor input. Alternatively, the script can be used by tutors
as lesson notes to guide their explanations to learners. If the
package is used for independent learning, it is recommended
that there should be opportunities for learner–tutor dialogue.
Dialogues should focus on errors in learners' thinking and on
learners' suggestions for altering algorithms. In the instructional
materials 'you' means the accounting learners.

INSTRUCTIONAL MATERIALS: ONE

Business scenario (1)

Bill had saved up £50, and he started up a stall at the Barrows which he called 'Melodia' and which sells second-hand tapes and discs. When someone starts up a business – even of the smallest kind like this stall at the Barrows – accountants talk about the business rather than the person owning it as the buyer and seller of goods and services. Bill is the owner of the business called 'Melodia' and he has lent it £50 to get started. This may seem an odd way of describing what is happening, but the rules of the accounting system do not work unless you regard the owner of the business – Bill – and the business – Melodia – as two different people. All the transactions you record are therefore the transactions of Melodia.

Because Melodia is a separate 'person' from Bill, he puts the £50 cash in a cash box marked 'Melodia'.

Melodia then bought 120 tapes for £60 from a shop that was closing down – 'Tunes'. The tapes can be paid for at the end of May; that is, the tapes were bought on credit. (Notice that you say that Melodia bought the tapes – obviously Bill did the actual buying but it was on behalf of Melodia – the tapes were not for his personal use.)

Melodia also bought records from various people who brought their unwanted discs to the Melodia stall. Altogether the business acquired 50 discs for £20, which Bill paid for in cash out of Melodia's cash box,

By the end of March, Melodia had sold all the stock of tapes and discs which it had bought. It sold 50 of the tapes to Deans Youth Club for £75 and they will pay Melodia at the end of April. The rest of the tapes were sold for £100 cash, which Bill put into Melodia's cash box. The discs were sold for £40; again, it was put into the cash box. (The bank account is introduced later in the materials.)

Figure 10.2 Collating simple accounting data

Fill in the following figures:
   Total amount of Melodia's sales   £ _____
   Total amount of Melodia's purchases   £ _____

   Gross profit made by Melodia
     during the month of March   £ _____

You can now understand what information you need to record if the financial records are to serve the first purpose – to know if the business is making a profit – and how much.

From the previous exercises you should be able to list the two pieces of information which have to be recorded to meet this purpose:

1

2

You can now go on to consider the second purpose: for the business to know if it can pay its debts as they fall due. This question has to be broken down into sub-questions:

(a) How do debts arise in a business? i.e., how does the business come to be owing money?
(b) Where does the money come from for a business to pay its debts?

To answer these questions it is necessary first of all to explain a basic distinction in financial transactions – between cash and credit transactions. (This distinction is explained in another section of the learning material which is not reproduced in this chapter.)

In the next exercise for the Melodia business you are going to identify:

1 amount owed by the business to trade creditors; and
2 amounts owed by customers (trade debtors) to the business.

In order to identify amounts owed to trade creditors ask yourself the question: what kind of transaction results in the business owing money to suppliers? To identify amounts owed to the business by trade debtors, ask yourself the question: what kind of transaction results in customers owing money to the business?

To help you to connect all the new points you have been learning, make a summary of the information you have worked out about Melodia's transactions by filling in the following figures:

Figure 10.3 Interpreting simple accounting data

How much does Melodia owe to its owner (Bill)?   £ _____
How much profit did Melodia make?   £ _____
The amount which Melodia owes to trade creditors is £ _____

> It will be able to pay this amount because:
>
> In its cash box Melodia has   £ _____
> and it is waiting to receive from its trade debtors   £ _____
>
> The amount due from trade debtors is due
> at the end of _____
>
> The amount due to trade creditors is due to be paid
> at the end of _____
>
> Supposing Melodia has only £20 in the cash box. Could Melodia still hope to pay the creditors in time? If so, why?

Notes for tutors

You would be expected to discuss the students' answers to the questions in a way which helped them to identify errors in their thinking. The students could also be shown how to construct simple algorithms which capture the thinking required for these exercises. Another similar exercise would be presented to the students based on a second business scenario.

The double-entry principle is then introduced in the materials, but no ledger entries are shown at this point (see page 178). Instead, the students are asked to look again at the first business scenario (Melodia), about which they answered questions (see Figure 10.3). The students will then be asked to identify two aspects of each transaction and to identify both of the aspects under the headings in Figure 10.4.

In a conventional 'lesson' this would probably be done in conjunction with tutor-led questioning and an overhead projector. The same question would be used for each transaction – namely, under which two headings of Figure 10.4 would you record this transaction?

Instructional materials: two is an example of the tutor's script or learners' text at this point.

INSTRUCTIONAL MATERIALS: TWO – TUTOR SCRIPT OR TEXT FOR LEARNERS

Remember that the script is designed for either tutor delivery or for reading by the learner. The information from the worksheets just completed for Melodia's transactions (Figures 10.2 and 10.3) has been rearranged in Figure 10.4 onto one page. Collecting the

Figure 10.4 Summarising Melodia's transactions

Amount which Melodia owed to its owner	Amount of each purchase	Amount of each sale	Each amount owed by the business to creditors	Each amount owed to the business by debtors	Each amount which went into the cash box	Each amount which went out of the cash box
£	£	£	£	£	£	£
	60		60		50	20
	20	75		75	100	
50		100			40	
		40				

headings together helps you to see the whole picture of Melodia's transactions.

The double-entry principle in accounting

You are now ready to take another step forward in your knowledge of the accounting system. So far, the example has been about 'a transaction', and the last transaction described for Melodia's business was:

the discs were sold for £40 – it was put into the cash box.

Our everyday understanding is that this sentence describes one transaction – a sale for cash. However, although the accounting system also sees this as one transaction, it treats the transaction as having two aspects to it:

1 some of the stock of goods which the business holds has been sold for £40 – that is, the business no longer holds these goods;
2 as a result of this sale, £40 has come into the cash box.

The accounting system views all financial transactions as having two aspects – that is, two sides to each transaction, two faces. If you look back at your work on Figures 10.2 and 10.3 you will see that you have in fact taken account of these two aspects of every transaction – although in your own work, the headings are on different pages instead of being collected together on the one page. For example, you can see that the £40 for the above transactions is included under one heading in Figure 10.2 and under another heading in Figure 10.3. Write the two headings below.

1 _____

and

2 _____

Go back to the description of Melodia's transactions on page 168.
    Read the first 13 lines – down to 'cash box marked Melodia'. This describes Bill lending £50 to Melodia and putting the £50 into Melodia's cash box. Now look again at Figure 10.4.
    Which two headings does this £50 appear under in Figure 10.4?

1 _____

and

2 _____

Notes for tutors

The learning materials (or the tutor) would continue by asking the students to identify the two headings under which each of Melodia's transactions appear in Figure 10.4.

Notes for tutors

The students are then asked to complete a worksheet similar to Figure 10.5 for another four to six business scenarios, with each scenario introducing a new transaction until all the common transactions such as goods returned inwards and outwards, expenses, purchases and sales of assets have been covered. The students are issued with copies of the worksheet shown in Figure 10.5 which has headings to accommodate these additional trans-actions. The students would be guided through the completion of the first scenario.

INSTRUCTIONAL MATERIALS: THREE – TUTOR SCRIPT OR TEXT FOR LEARNERS

Business scenario (2)

You started up Runsports by lending it £2,000 which was placed in an account marked 'Runsports' at the Bank of Scotland.

Runsports paid by cheque £300 for a new counter and display stand which it bought.

It also bought a till at £100 and paid by cheque.

Runsports also bought in running shoes and shorts at a total cost of £1,200, which it paid for by cheque.

During the month Runsports sold all of this stock for cash – £2,500 – and it paid all of this cash into its account at the Bank of Scotland.

The first transaction of Runsports is the one which brought Runsports into existence as a business:

Runsports received a loan of £2,000 from you and this went into Runsports' account at the bank.

We have to identify the two aspects of this transaction:

1 How can we describe the first of these two aspects of the business? Runsports' owner (you) gave it a loan of £2,000: therefore the business called 'Runsports' owes £2,000 to the owner (you).

Figure 10.5 A summary sheet for recurring transactions

Amount of each item of stock purchased	Each item of stock retnd to spplrs	Amount of each item of stock sold	Each item of stock retnd by customers	Amount of each asset purchased	Each amount which went into the bank	Each amount which went out of the bank	Each amount which went into the till cash	Each amount which went out of the till cash	Each change in amount owed by the business to creditors		Each change in amount owed to the business by debtors		Each expense paid
									Inc in amount owed	Dec in amount owed	Inc in amount owed	Dec in amount owed	
£	£	£	£	£	£	£	£	£					
							50						

Total

Total owed by the business to the owner = £50

2 How can we describe the second of these two aspects? £2,000
went into the business's account at the bank.

You can see that this has been entered under the appropriate
headings on the sheet.

You should now enter each of Runsports transactions under
two headings. The first step is to ask yourself the same two
questions in relation to each transaction. (Write your answers
under the questions.)

What is the first aspect of the transaction?

What is the second aspect of this transaction?

What are the two appropriate headings on the worksheet?
(Figure 10.5)

Notes for tutors

The students are given the sheet in Figure 10.7 with self-questions
(Figure. 10.6) in order to form correct mental operations. The
students are asked to connect together the concepts they have
been using by completing key relations charts (Figure 10.7).

Figure 10.6 Procedural questions for ledger entries

Proceed as follows:

1 Read each transaction listed across the top of the chart: the
first transaction reads:
   Purchased goods for cash.
2 Represent this transaction to yourself in words and/or a
diagram, whichever you find easier.
   To help you to do this, ask yourself questions like these:
   • Does the business have more of – or less of – something? If
   so, what does the business have more of or less of?
   • What events have actually happened? e.g., goods might
   have come back to the business.
   • What is the effect on the business of what has happened?
   e.g., if it gets goods in and does not pay immediately, it
   owes someone.
3 Read the description of the result of the transaction in the left-
hand column (result of transaction).
4 Select the descriptions which best describe the result of this
transaction and place ticks against these descriptions.
5 Repeat steps 1–4 for the other three transactions.

Figure 10.7 Effects of transactions

Place a tick in the appropriate boxes in the chart.

Result of transaction	Purchased goods for cash	Sold goods for cash	Purchased goods on credit	Sold goods on credit	Customer returned goods he had bought on credit from you	Your bus. rt'd goods it had bought on credit to supplr.	Customer paid amount he owes you	Your bus. paid amount it owed to supplr.
Cash/cheques come into the business								
Cash/cheques go out of the business								
Stock comes into the business								
Stock goes out of the business								
The business owes more to creditors								
Debtors owe more to the business								
The business owes less to creditors								
Debtors owe less to the business								

Notes for tutors

It is only at this point that ledger accounts are introduced. Instructional materials (set four) show the beginning of a tutor script or learners' text which explains how worksheets in the form of Figures 10.4 and 10.5 develop into ledger accounts.

INSTRUCTIONAL MATERIALS FOUR: TUTOR SCRIPT OR TEXT FOR STUDENTS

Connecting the worksheets with ledger accounts

It has been stresssed that transactions are recorded for a purpose: to answer two basic questions about the business:

1 Has it made a profit – if so, how much?
2 Can it pay its debts when they are due – and where will the money come from?

In all the exercises you have completed you were able to provide all the information to answer these questions by:

(a) reading the description of each transaction;
(b) identifying its two aspects;
(c) noting these two aspects under the appropriate two headings on the worksheet.

An accounting system works in much the same way as these worksheet exercises you have just done. The only real difference is that the accounting system uses a more complicated layout than the headed worksheets. It is quite a small step for you to move from recording the transactions of a business as you have been doing on the worksheets to recording them in the special layout which is called an accounting system.

Why is an accounting system needed? In other words, why could we not just continue to record transactions on the headed worksheets?

There are usually far more transactions in a real business than you dealt with in the exercises. It would be difficult to calculate the information you are interested in from the worksheets if there is a large number of transactions.

The most important part of the special layout used in accounting is called the ledger. Go back to Figure 10.4, which is the completed worksheet for Melodia's transactions. Compare Figure 10.4 with Figure 10.9, which shows how Melodia's transactions would be laid out on a ledger page of an accounting system. Look at the ledger pages as you read these notes below:

Notes

The same headings have been used as those on the worksheet, except that the heading has been shortened to one word – such as 'purchases'.

The word 'account' (usually abbreviated to 'a/c') is written after the heading word. An a/c in a ledger simply means a list – or package of information – about whatever the heading is describing. An a/c serves just the same purpose as each heading on the worksheets you have been using.

The name of the creditors – Tunes – and the name of the debtors – Deans Youth Club – appear as a/c headings instead of just a heading of creditor and debtor as appeared on the worksheets.

Why do you think the name of the creditor or debtor should be at the top of the a/c?

Remember that each transaction has two aspects.

Remember that you always noted each transaction under two headings.

Exactly the same happens in the ledger. Each transaction appears in two a/cs.

In fact, each a/c tells you about the other aspect of the transaction. The worksheets did not tell you this piece of information, although you could work it out.

Take Melodia's ledger (Figure 10.9) and complete the sentences in Figure 10.8 to check that you have understood these points:

Figure 10.8 Checking the application of the double-entry principle

The £50 in the owner's Capital a/c is also recorded in the . . . . a/c.
The £60 in the Purchases a/c is also recorded in the. . . . . a/c.
The £100 and the £40 in the Sales a/c are also recorded
   in the . . . . a/c.
The £60 in the Tunes a/c is also recorded in the . . . . a/c.
The £75 in the Deans a/c is also recorded in the. . . . . a/c.
The £50 in the Cash a/c is also recorded in the. . . . . a/c.
The £100 and the £40 in the Cash a/c are also
   recorded in the. . . . . a/c.
The £20 in the Cash a/c is also recorded in the. . . . . a/c.

The information in Figure 10.9 is exactly the same as that shown in Figure 10.4 (except for the addition of dates in Figure 10.9). The only significant difference between Figure 10.4 and 10.9 is the layout.

Figure 10.9 Melodia's ledger

General ledger

		DR £	CR £	Balance DR £	CR £

Sales account

March	7	Deans Youth Club		75		
	14	Cash		100		
	25	Cash		40		

Purchases account

| March | 2 | Tunes | 60 | | | |
| | 10 | Cash | 20 | | | |

Cash account

March	1	Capital	50			
	10	Purchases		20		
	14	Sales	100			
	25		40			

Capital account

| March | 1 | Cash | | 50 | | |

Sales ledger (debtors' ledger)

Deans Youth Club account

| March | 7 | Sales | 75 | | | |

Purchases ledger (Creditors' ledger)

Tunes account

| March | 2 | Purchases | | 60 | | |

We now come to an important difference between your simple worksheets and the ledger page.

There are always two money columns in the ledger for each account:

1 one column is called the Debit side – usually abbreviated to dr.
2 one column is called the Credit side – usually abbreviated to cr.

In Figure 10.9 you will see that the debit column is placed on the left of the credit column.

When you recorded the transactions on the worksheets the headings were not split into a debit column and a credit column as they are on the ledger. There are good reasons for allowing each account to have a debit and credit side. The accounting system has rules about:

1 what can be recorded on the debit side; and
2 what can be recorded on the credit side.

The two sides (debit and credit), plus the rules about what can be written on each side, enable you to read off much more information from the accounts in the ledger than you could read off from the worksheet headings you have been using so far. This point will only become clear to you when you have done the next few exercises.

One more difference: some of the accounts are on a page marked General ledger; others are on a page marked Creditors' ledger or Debtors' ledger.

It is useful to split up the ledger into these three sections. It allows you to see at once all the debtors' accounts or all the creditors' accounts – or all the accounts relating to purchases, sales and cash or bank.

To help you understand the above points, answer the questions in Figure 10.10 about the accounts in Melodia's ledger: identifying ledger entries for purchases, sales, debtors and creditors:

Figure 10.10 Identifying ledger entries

On which side – debit or credit – are the entries
which tell you how much
Melodia purchased during the month?   _____

On which side is the entry which tells
you how much Melodia owes to Tunes?   _____

On which side is the entry which tells
you how much Melodia sold during the
month?

_____

On which side is the entry which tells
you how much Deans Youth Club
owes to Melodia?

_____

There is also a column headed Balance in Figure 10.9. The use of this will be explained later. It is a summarising column.

Notes for tutors

The rules for deciding whether an entry should be in the debit or credit side of an account can be stated in different ways; for example, in terms of three different types of accounts or in terms of whether the transaction increases or decreases an asset or a liability. Whatever way the rules are described they should be illustrated by reference to the worksheets in the form of Figure 10.5 already completed by students. This has the advantage that the transactions and headings which describe each aspect of the transaction are familiar to the students. Some of the difficulties students experience may arise from having to process too much new information at once.

After the rules for debit and credit entries in ledger accounts are explained and illustrated, the students are asked to develop a simple algorithm for applying these rules. The algorithm is best constructed through tutor-led questioning and discussion of student suggestions. It is then used when the students are practising applying the rules in a number of exercises. Figures 10.11 and 10.12 show two alternative algorithms which set out the mental operations for deciding whether a ledger account should have a debit or a credit entry for any particular transaction. These algorithms were developed by students during tutor-led guided discussion. Either of the algorithms will lead to a correct debit or credit decision if the questions are answered correctly. Before using the second algorithm in Figure 10.12, 'Personal Account' would have been defined as a debtor or creditor account and 'Nominal Accounts' would have been defined as accounts recording expenses and gains.

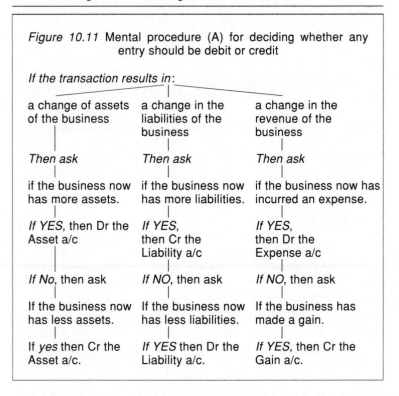

Figure 10.11 Mental procedure (A) for deciding whether any entry should be debit or credit

If the transaction results in:

a change of assets of the business	a change in the liabilities of the business	a change in the revenue of the business
Then ask	*Then ask*	*Then ask*
if the business now has more assets.	if the business now has more liabilities.	if the business now has incurred an expense.
If YES, then Dr the Asset a/c	*If YES,* then Cr the Liability a/c	*If YES,* then Dr the Expense a/c
If No, then ask	*If NO,* then ask	*If NO,* then ask
If the business now has less assets.	If the business now has less liabilities.	If the business has made a gain.
If *yes* then Cr the Asset a/c.	*If YES* then Dr the Liability a/c.	*If YES,* then Cr the Gain a/c.

The instructional materials in this chapter are extracts from a much larger set of materials. In between each extract in the complete set are other instructional materials which facilitate a gradual build-up of a conceptual framework.

PREPARING A PROFIT AND LOSS ACCOUNT AND A BALANCE SHEET

The materials were provided by Mairearad Kirkland, a lecturer at Bell College, Hamilton. They were designed as guidelines for tutors but could be used for independent learning supported by tutor feedback.

Students often take longer than they should to learn to prepare simple final accounts from a list of account balances in the trial balance. One reason is that the layout of final accounts is introduced before the purpose has been understood, and the students'

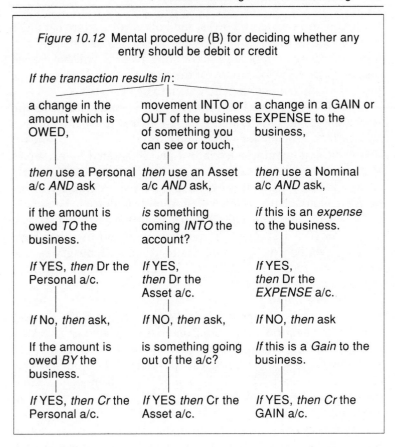

Figure 10.12 Mental procedure (B) for deciding whether any entry should be debit or credit

If the transaction results in:

a change in the amount which is OWED,	movement INTO or OUT of the business of something you can see or touch,	a change in a GAIN or EXPENSE to the business,
then use a Personal a/c *AND* ask	*then* use an Asset a/c *AND* ask,	*then* use a Nominal a/c *AND* ask,
if the amount is owed *TO* the business.	*is* something coming *INTO* the account?	*if* this is an *expense* to the business.
If YES, *then* Dr the Personal a/c.	*If* YES, *then* Dr the Asset a/c.	*If* YES, *then* Dr the *EXPENSE* a/c.
If No, *then* ask,	*If* NO, *then* ask,	*If* NO, *then* ask
If the amount is owed *BY* the business.	is something going out of the a/c?	*If* this is a *Gain* to the business.
If YES, *then* *Cr* the Personal a/c.	*If* YES *then* Cr the Asset a/c.	*If* YES, *then* *Cr* the GAIN a/c.

attention is so taken up with the details of the layout that conceptual understanding is squeezed out. In the approach which follows, the emphasis is on understanding the relevant concepts before these are applied to the task of preparing the final accounts. The major categories of accounts which would have been highlighted by using the approach suggested in the previous section are asset, liability, capital, income, expenditure.

Notes for tutors

The main purposes of drawing up summary statements (Trading and Profit and Loss Account and Balance Sheet) would be explained – to highlight net profit and its components; to show what a business owns and owes, and how easily current liabilities can be met. If the approach in the previous section has been followed, these purposes of accounting records will have been discussed from the beginning of the course and only the specific form of the final accounts will remain to be mastered.

It would be explained that the asset and liability categories are now going to be sub-divided – the assets into fixed and current, and the liabilities into long-term and current. The main features of these concepts would be explained and illustrated by examples and non-examples of each. For example, the main feature of a current liability is that it is expected to be paid within a year; an example is a bank overdraft, a non-example is a loan to be re-paid in five years' time. The main features of current assets is that they can be converted into cash in the short term and that they have varying degrees of liquidity. Students should be given this information about the features of the new concepts on a printed sheet for easy reference.

Before beginning to prepare final accounts, students should be given a list of account names and asked to classify them under the above categories and sub-categories as a way of checking that accounting concepts have been understood. Figure 10.13 shows an exercise sheet for this purpose. After the students have checked their own classification they should engage in class discussion with regard to any wrongly classified accounts in order to clarify misconceptions. As a further check on under-standing of double-entry principles, they should then be asked to return to the list of account names and write opposite each account whether it would have a debit or credit balance. Again, after self-checking, there should be discussion aimed at exploring reasons for wrong answers.

A copy of the Trial Balance in Figure 10.14 would then be given to students, and they would be asked to write against each account in the list the category to which it belongs (that is, current or fixed asset, current or long-term liability, capital, income, expenditure). As before, students would check their own work and explore misconceptions through dialogue.

Students would then be given the sample layouts in Figures 10.16 and 10.17 for a Trading and Profit and Loss Account and for a Balance Sheet. In these sample layouts the tutor has the numbers 1–4 in the left-hand margin to help the students match the layout to the algorithm in Figure 10.15. Students working in small

Figure 10.13 Classifying accounts

Account	Asset Fixed curr	Liability Long-term curr	Income	Expense	Capital	Profit & Loss a/c	Balance sheet	Why
Machinery								
Rent								
Bank O/D								
Creditors								
Stock								
Premises								
Capital								
Debtors								
Interest rec'd								
Discount all'd								
Wages								
Sales								
Purchases								
Vehicles								
Cash								
5-year loan from M.E.								
Accrued Tax								
Advertising								
Furniture								
Prepaid ins.								

Figure 10.14 Trial balance

Account name	Dr £	Cr £
Premises	220,000	
Sales		130,000
Wages	35,000	
Fixtures	80,000	
Debtors (SLC)	15,000	
Creditors (PLC)		6,000
Vehicles	48,000	
Insurance	3,000	
Bank	7,000	
Cash	1,000	
Rent receivable		5,000
Purchases	75,000	
Heat & light	4,000	
Motor expenses	3,000	
General expenses	5,000	
Loan from		25,000
Capital		330,000
	496,000	496,000

groups are unlikely to discover quickly an efficient algorithm for preparing final accounts, so it is probably better to copy the algorithm in Figure 10.15 onto a transparency and to show it on an overhead projector.

For each item in the trial balance a different student would be asked to talk aloud the path through the algorithm, answering each question. Students would then enter the item in the sample layouts in the place indicated by the algorithm. Because the students are likely to be seeking clarification of some points, discussion would take place. This algorithm could have additional questions to highlight the important aspects of the thinking procedure. For example, after 'expense' there could have been the question 'Does this decrease or increase profit?' rather than simply telling the answer.

Students would go on to practise preparing final accounts from other trial balances, the items becoming gradually more complex. If the algorithm needs to be altered to accommodate more complex

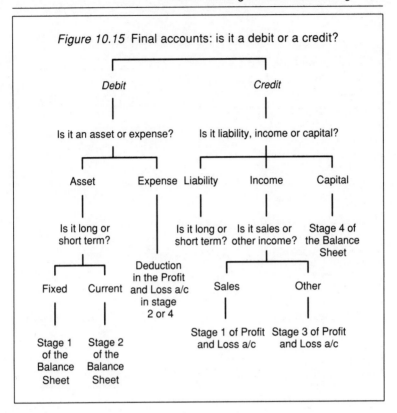

Figure 10.15 Final accounts: is it a debit or a credit?

examples, the alteration could be the subject of discussion with the students. Several copies of the algorithm should be given to each student so that the steps can be ticked until they can easily remember the procedure. If time permits, students should be encouraged to construct their own algorithms for future work.

FURTHER READING

The instructional materials in pages 164–83 are extracts from R. Soden (1990) 'An experimental course of instruction: introduction to principles of accounts', an appendix to an unpublished PhD thesis 'The improvement of adult cognitive performance'. Enquiries about the set of materials should be made to the author in the Faculty of Education, University of Strathclyde, Glasgow.

Figure 10.16 Sample layout

Trading and Profit and Loss Account of _____
for the year ended _____

1

Sales

2

Less cost of sales

= Gross Profit/Loss

3

Add other income

4

Less expenses

= Net Profit/Loss

Figure 10.17 Sample layout

Balance Sheet of _____
As at _____

1

Fixed assets

2

Current assets

Less current liabilities

= NET current assets

3

Less long-term liabilities

£ _____

4

Financed by:

£ _____

Appendix
A background to theory and research

You may find it useful to read the following reports which give a flavour of experimental work which has been based on the principles explained in this book.

In the 1950s and 1960s, when American researchers were using computer simulation to produce descriptions of the mental processes involved in problem solving, researchers in the USSR, directed by Landa, were also working on descriptions of these processes but based the research on experimental work with school students. The aim of the prodigious Russian programmes (Landa 1974, 1976) was to produce descriptions of mental actions from which instructional prescriptions could be derived. These would result in achievement gains by students in various secondary school subjects; impressive gains have been demonstrated, particularly in geometry and Russian grammar.

Landa started from the premise that people can be taught to think well, and the ultimate aim of his research is to produce a theory to account for the learning of concept structures and mental operations/procedures, of how these may generate further cognitive development and to connect this theory to instructional procedures. The elements of the theory at present are similar to the models of problem solving produced by British and American researchers. Landa's account of mental operations arises from a part of the research programme which aims to improve students' achievements in geometry problems. The experimental and control groups were composed of students whose teachers attributed their failure to make progress to lack of aptitude or intelligence, but Landa hypothesised that the failure was due to lack of instruction in the 'general procedures of thinking'. Before instruction, 25 per cent of the problems were solved; after instruction, 87 per cent were solved. Landa hypothesised that since the mental procedures taught had been general enough to improve performance in various classes of geometry problems, it would be possible to identify and teach mental procedures for other subject matter. Procedures were evolved for the solution of certain kinds of grammatical problems and taught to students. This resulted in a much more striking improvement in achievements. The number of grammatical mistakes made by students decreased seven-fold (Landa 1961, 1964). The much greater improvement was attributed to the fact that it is possible to specify to a much greater extent the procedures required in grammatical problems. In geometry it was not found possible to specify procedures unequivocally and therefore fully. In some subjects it will be possible to construct fuller procedures than in others.

A number of researchers who have looked at problem solving in geometry and in other subject matters have reached similar conclusions. According to these researchers, mental procedures are rarely explicitly presented in British and American instructional material, and most teachers do not explicitly identify this kind of knowledge when they teach. They suggest that students who acquire mental procedures to a satisfactory degree often do so by induction – from looking at solutions to sample problems and following the steps the tutor demonstrates when working out problems. An early study (Gagné and Smith 1962), which attempted to teach such procedures explicitly, found that students asked to justify each of their moves before making it performed better than students not given this instruction.

It is in connecting this theory with instructional procedures that Landa's research makes an important contribution to curriculum planning. Gagné and Dick (1983) characterised Landa's ideas as 'precise definition of procedures to be taught and the presentation and explication of these procedures to the student in the clearest and most direct possible manner'. As noted, it is important to stress that 'direct' does not imply a mechanistic approach to instruction, but rather one which fosters in the students development of complex insights into the nature of thinking itself. Proper instruction requires a presentation which allows students to discover mental operations and procedures under the guidance of the teacher. According to Landa, one of the mechanisms by which mental operations became transferable to general reasoning ability is through the insight developed by students in the course of this guided discovery into the nature of knowledge and the mental operations required to master it. Many examples of attempts to develop such insight are found in Landa's prodigious research. At one stage of his research, before children are introduced to specific mental procedures, several hours are spent guiding them towards discovery of the nature of concepts. In teaching mental procedures for solving classes of geometry problems, the instructional programme begins by discussions on the nature of the process of proving anything, of making students aware of general operations. The programme then goes on to discussion of how solutions to the class of problems were made up of operations in a particular sequence. Landa's data show not only an increase in the number of problems solved correctly, but also a change in the thinking process which occurred during their solution. The development of such insights are hypothesised to facilitate transfer to new tasks.

A rigorous, large-scale Dutch study (Assink 1987) compared a type of explicit instruction in mental procedures inspired by Landa's work with a method termed 'analogy'. The content of the instruction – the complex rules of verb orthography – was the most difficult aspect of Dutch orthography. The analogy method seeks to avoid overburdening the student with grammatical terminology and rules. It is based on the idea of teaching orthography by selecting a limited number of specimen verbs that serve as models or prototypes of the various conjugation classes occurring in the Dutch language. The analogy method can be characterised as an approach in which the student is taught to apply orthographic rules in such a way that these rules are left more or less implicit. This teaching approach was justified by the generally accepted conviction among educators that the application of grammatical rules and concepts is too difficult for children of elementary school age. Nation-wide Dutch studies in educational achievement suggested that the results of the analogy method left much to be desired. Assink set out to specify and teach explicitly the sequence of mental operations that must be performed to arrive at correct orthographic decisions. The main difference between the algorithmic approach and the analogy method is that the former enables the students to determine unequivocally the grammatical and morphological properties of the target verb in order to arrive at the correct spelling decision.

Many of the features of the instructional situation were consistent with the instructional work reviewed above. The last steps are the automatising and subsequently abbreviating of the sequence of decision steps into shorter problem-solving sequences, and finally solving orthography problems without the help of the algorithm. The learners in the experimental group significantly outperformed those in the control group.

A series of studies, which make an outstanding contribution to understanding how instruction needs to be organised if it is to promote problem-solving abilities in knowledge-rich domains, are those carried out by researchers at the University of Twente. Their initial aim was to improve the ability of first-year degree students to solve the thermodynamic problems presented in the first year course. Subsequently, they extended their research to the domain of public administration policy design, aiming to develop courses to improve students' problem solving.

These researchers set out to identify the most useful mental procedures for tackling the classes of thermodynamics problems which their first-year students were expected to master. They found that the lecturers in the course and other specialists could not give an adequate description of mental operations. Other researchers confirm that tutors are largely unable to describe such operations or procedures explicitly, and some have suggested that improving teachers' knowledge of such operations through explicit instruction may make an important contribution to improving students' performance. Various attempts were made to construct what the Netherlands team called PAM (Programme of Action and Methods), using thinking-aloud protocols from staff and students, research literature on special heuristics and on PAMs for other subject matter, plus research on errors that are frequently made in students' work. The PAM eventually produced was too complicated for student use, and it had to be converted to what researchers called a SAP (Systematic Approach to Problem Solving). The SAP chart contained only mental operations unknown to the students and which were strictly necessary for solving the most important problems.

The SAP charts produced for the student were incorporated into a wider instructional plan which made provision for integrating the body of concepts being learned. This was done by drawing students' attention repeatedly to the most important relationships between concepts which arise from laws and formulae in thermodynamics. The researchers argue that in order to make the necessary inferences to solve problems, students must be able to retrieve easily these 'key relations' and the conditions for their use. This is supported by other research, which suggests that good problem solvers had their subject-matter knowledge organised around key principles, and these principles were connected in structures by key relationships. It is the instructional procedure that is of particular interest. After a few lectures on a given topic, the students were asked to produce a summary of the key relations for that topic in the form of a chart. These were discussed and then compared with the instructor's own key relations charts. Students used the key relations charts continuously during the problem-solving exercises and the instructors referred to the charts when giving feedback. This is, of course, consistent with the approach presented throughout this book.

Terlouw and Mettes (1984) had also investigated the possibility of specifying and teaching to students optimum mental activities for solving policy design problems set in connection with their courses in Town Renovation and EEC Agriculture Policy. This research is still in progress, but so far there is evidence that the researchers have been able to construct mental procedures which correspond sufficiently closely to the actual activities of experts in these fields. A questionnaire analysis shows that the Systematic Problem Approach (SPA) derived from this model was rated by students as useful and desirable. At present work is still being done on how students can best be instructed in the use of the SPA.

FURTHER READING

Assink, E. M. (1987) 'Algorithms in spelling instruction: the orthography of Dutch verbs', *Journal of Educational Psychology* 79 (3): 228–35.

Mettes, C., Pilot, A. and Roosink, H. J. (1981) 'Linking factual and procedural knowledge in solving science problems', *Instructional Science* 10 (4): 333–61.

Terlouw, C. and Mettes, C. T. (1984) 'A systematic problem approach for designing policy: validation by experts and students', *Doc 84–12*, Educational Centre, University of Twente.

REFERENCES

Gagné, R. M. and Dick, W. (1983) 'Instructional psychology', *Annual Review of Psychology* 34: 261–95.

Gagné, R. M. and Smith, E.C. (1962) 'A study of the effects of verbalisation on problem solving', *Journal of Experimental Psychology* 63: 12–18.

Landa, L. (1961, 1964) in *Instructional Regulation and Control*, L. Landa (ed.) Englewood Cliffs, NJ: Educational Technology Publications (1976).

—— (1974) *Algorithmization in Learning and Instruction*, Englewood Cliffs, NJ: Educational Technology Publications.

Index